Autumn Knits

www.bernat.com

very effort has been taken to ensure the accuracy of these instructions.
ernat®, however, cannot accept responsibility for typographical errors or m

T0405488

1. Weekend Cardigan and Beret

CIRCULAR NEEDLE

BERET: DOUBLE-POINTED NEEDLES

SUPER BULKY

INTERMEDIATE

SIZES

Cardigan

To fit bust measurement
Extra-Small/Small 28-34" [71-86.5 cm]
Medium 36-38" [91.5-96.5 cm]
Large 40-42" [101.5-106.5 cm]
Extra-Large 44-46" [112-117 cm]
2/3 Extra-Large 48-54" [122-137 cm]
4/5 Extra-Large 56-62" [142-157.5 cm]

Finished bust	
Extra-Small/Small:	36" [91.5 cm]
Medium:	40" [101.5 cm]
Large:	44" [112 cm]
Extra-Large:	48" [122 cm]
2/3 Extra-Large:	55" [139.5 cm]
4/5 Extra-Large:	63" [160 cm]

Beret: One size to fit average lady's head.

GAUGE

11 sts and 14 rows = 4" [10 cm] with large needles in stocking st.

ABBREVIATIONS

See page 65 for Helpful Hints.

Alt = Alternate(ing).

Beg = Beginning.

C4B = Slip next 2 stitches onto cable needle and leave at back of work. K2, then K2 from cable needle.

C6B = Slip next 3 stitches onto a cable needle and leave at back of work. K3, then K3 from cable needle.

Cont = Continue(ity).

Dec = Decrease(ing).

Inc = Increase 1 stitch by knitting into front and back of next stitch.

K = Knit.

K2tog = Knit next 2 stitches together.

M1 = Make 1 stitch by picking up horizontal loop lying before next stitch and knitting into back of loop.

P = Purl.

P2tog = Purl next 2 stitches together.

Pat = Pattern.

Rem = Remaining.

Rep = Repeat.

Rnd(s) = Round(s).

RS = Right side.

Ssk = Slip next 2 stitches knitwise one at a time. Pass them back onto left-hand needle, then knit through back loops together.

St(s) = Stitch(es).

Tog = Together.

Work 2tog = K2tog or P2tog as they appear.

WS = Wrong side.

MATERIALS

Bernat® Softee® Chunky™ (100 g/3.5 oz; 99 m/108 yds)								
Cardigan	**Sizes**	**XS/S**	**M**	**L**	**XL**	**2/3XL**	**4/5XL**	
28522 (Redwood)		10	11	12	13	14	15	**balls**

Sizes 6.5 mm (U.S. 10½) and 8 mm (U.S. 11) knitting needles. Size 6.5 mm (U.S. 10½) circular knitting needle 24" [60 cm] long **or size needed to obtain gauge.** 1 st holder. Cable needle. 1 button.

Beret

28522 (Redwood) **1 ball**

Set of 4 sizes 6.5 mm (U.S. 10½) and 8 mm (U.S. 11) double-pointed knitting needles **or size needed to obtain gauge.** Cable needle.

INSTRUCTIONS

CARDIGAN

The instructions are written for smallest size. If changes are necessary for larger sizes the instructions will be written thus ( ). Numbers for each size are shown in the same color throughout the pattern. When only one number is given in black, it applies to all sizes.

BACK

With smaller needles, cast on **58** (**65-72-79-86-93**) sts.
1st row: (RS). P2. *K5. P2. Rep from * to end of row.
2nd row: K2. *P5. K2. Rep from * to end of row.
Rep last 2 rows of (K5. P2) ribbing once more.

Next row: (RS). P2. *K2. M1. K3. P2. Rep from * to end of row. **66** (**74-82-90-98-106**) sts.
Next row: K2. *(P1. K1) 3 times. K2. P6. K2. Rep from * to last **0** (**8-0-8-0-8**) sts. (K1. P1) **0** (**3-0-3-0-3**) times. K**0** (**2-0-2-0-2**).

Change to larger needles and proceed in pat as follows:
(See Chart I on page 12).
1st row: (RS). P2. (K1. P1) **0** (**3-0-3-0-3**) times. P**0** (**2-0-2-0-2**). *C6B. P2. (K1. P1) 3 times. P2. Rep from * to end of row.
2nd row: K2. *(P1. K1) 3 times. K2. P6. K2. Rep from * to last **0** (**8-0-8-0-8**) sts. (P1. K1) **0** (**3-0-3-0-3**) times. K**0** (**2-0-2-0-2**).
3rd row: P2. (K1. P1) **0** (**3-0-3-0-3**) times. P**0** (**2-0-2-0-2**). *K6. P2. (K1. P1) 3 times. K2. Rep from * to end of row.

4th to 11th rows: Rep 2nd and 3rd row 4 times more.
12th row: As 2nd row.
13th row: P2. K**0** (**8-0-8-0-8**). P**0** (**2-0-2-0-2**). *(K1. P1) 3 times. P2. C6B. P2. Rep from * to end of row.
14th row: K2. *P6. K2. (P1. K1) 3 times. K2. Rep from * to last **0** (**8-0-8-0-8**) sts. P**0** (**6-0-8-0-8**). K**0** (**2-0-2-0-2**).
15th row: P2. K**0** (**8-0-8-0-8**). P**0** (**2-0-2-0-2**). *(K1. P1) 3 times. P2. K6. P2. Rep from * to end of row.
16th to 23rd rows: As 14th and 15th row 4 times more.
24th row: As 14th row.
Rep 1st to 24th rows for pat, AT SAME TIME dec 1 st each end of needle on next and every following 6th row to **58** (**70-64-80-94-102**) sts, then every following 4th row to **50** (**56-60-74-76-88**) sts.

Cont even in pat until work from beg measures **19** (**19-20-20-20-19**)" [**48** (**48-51-51-51-48**) cm], ending with a WS row.

Shape sleeves: Cont in pat, inc 1 st each end of needle on next 5 rows, then every following alt row 3 times more, taking inc sts into pat. **66** (**72-76-90-92-104**) sts.
Next row: (WS). Work even in pat.
Cast on **10** (**12-12-12-12-8**) sts beg next 2 rows, taking inc sts into pat. **86** (**96-100-114-116-120**) sts. Place marker at end of last row.

ont even in pat until work from marked ow measures **11** (**12-12-13-14-14**)" [**28** **30.5-30.5-33-35.5-35.5**) cm], ending with WS row.

hape shoulders: Cast off **15** (**18-19-21-** **2-23**) sts beg next 2 rows, then **16** (**18-19-** **1-22-23**) sts beg next 2 rows.

eave rem **24** (**24-24-28-28-28**) sts on a st holder.

EFT FRONT

*With smaller needles, cast on **30** (**30-37-** **7-44-51**) sts.

st row: (RS). P2. *K5. P2. Rep from * to end of row.

2nd row: K2. *P5. K2. Rep from * to end of row.

Rep last 2 rows of (K7. P2) ribbing once more.

Next row: (RS). P2. *K2. M1. K3. P2. Rep from * to end of row. **34** (**34-42-42-50-** **8**) sts.**

Next row: K2. *(K1. P1) 3 times. K2. P6. K2. Rep from * to last **0** (**0-8-8-0-8**) sts. (K1. P1) **0** (**0-3-3-0-3**) times. K0 (**0-2-2-0-2**).

Change to larger needles and proceed in pat as follows:

1st row: (RS). P2. (K1. P1) **0** (**0-3-3-0-3**) times. P0 (**0-2-2-0-2**). *C6B. P2. (K1. P1) 3 times. P2. Rep from * to end of row.

2nd row: K2. *(P1. K1) 3 times. K2. P6. K2. Rep from * to last **0** (**0-8-8-0-8**) sts. (P1. K1) **0** (**0-3-3-0-3**) times. K0 (**0-2-2-0-2**).

3rd row: P2. (K1. P1) **0** (**0-3-3-0-3**) times. K0 (**0-2-2-0-2**).*(K1. P1) 3 times. K2. P8. K2. Rep from * to end of row.

4th to 11th rows: Rep 2nd and 3rd rows 4 times more.

12th row: As 2nd row.

13th row: P2. (C6B) **0** (**0-1-1-0-1**) time. P0 (**0-2-2-0-2**). *(K1. P1) 3 times. P2. C6B. P2. Rep from * to end of row.

14th row: K2. *P6. K2. (P1. K1) 3 times. K2. Rep from * to last **0** (**0-8-8-0-8**) sts. P0 (**0-6-6-0-6**). K0 (**0-2-2-0-2**).

15th row: P2. K0 (**0-6-6-0-6**). P0 (**0-2-2-0-2**). *(K1. P1) 3 times. P2. K6. K2. Rep from * to end of row.

16th to 23rd rows: As 14th and 15th rows 4 times more.

24th row: As 14th row.

Rep 1st to 24th rows for pat, AT SAME TIME, dec 1 st at beg of needle on next and every following 6th row to **28** (**29-40-36-48-56**) sts, then every following 4th row to **26** (**28-32-34-39-49**) sts.

Cont even in pat until work from beg measures **19** (**19-20-20-20-19**)" [**48** (**48-51-51-51-48**) cm], ending with a RS row.

Shape front placket: 1st row: (WS). Cast off 11 sts. Pat to end of row. **15** (**17-21-23-28-38**) sts.

Shape sleeve and V-neck edge: Cont in pat, proceed as follows:

1st row: (RS). Inc 1 st in first st. Pat to end of row.

2nd row: Pat to last 2 sts. Inc 1 st in next st. K1.

Rep last 2 rows once more. **19** (**21-25-27-32-42**) sts.

Proceed as follows:

1st row: (RS). Inc 1 st in first st. Pat to end of row.

2nd row: Work even in pat.

Rep last 2 rows 3 times more. **23** (**25-29-31-36-46**) sts.

Next row: (RS). Cast on **10** (**12-12-12-12-8**) sts. Pat to end of row. **33** (**37-41-43-48-54**) sts.

Next row: Work even in pat. Place marker at end of last row.

Next row: (RS). Pat to last 3 sts. Work 2tog. K1 (V-neck edge).

Work **17** (**0-11-0-7-3**) rows even.

Rep last **18** (**0-12-0-8-4**) rows **1** (**0-2-0-3-7**) time(s) more. **31** (**36-38-42-44-46**) sts.

Cont even in pat until work from marked row measures **11** (**12-12-13-14-14**)" [**28** (**30.5-30.5-33-35.5-35.5**) cm], ending with a WS row.

Shape shoulder: Cast off **15** (**18-19-21-22-23**) sts beg of next row. Work 1 row even. Cast off rem **16** (**18-19-21-22-23**) sts.

Work from ** to ** as given for Left Front.

Next row: K**0** (**0-2-2-0-2**). (K1. P1) **0** (**0-3-3-0-3**) times. K2. *P6. K2. (K1. P1) 3 times. K2. Rep from * to end of row.

Change to larger needles and proceed in pat as follows:

1st row: (RS). P2. *(K1. P1) 3 times. P2. C6B. P2. Rep from * to last **0** (**0-8-8-0-8**) sts. (K1. P1) **0** (**0-3-3-0-3**) times. P**0** (**0-2-2-0-2**).

2nd row: K**0** (**0-2-2-0-2**). (P1. K1) **0** (**0-3-3-0-3**) times. K2. *P6. K2. (P1. K1) 3 times. K2. Rep from * to end of row.

3rd row: P2. *(K1. P1) 3 times. P2. K6. P2. Rep from * to last **0** (**0-8-8-0-8**) sts. (K1. P1) **0** (**0-3-3-0-3**) times. P**0** (**0-2-2-0-2**).

4th to 11th rows: Rep 2nd and 3rd rows 4 times more.

12th row: As 2nd row.

13th row: P2. *C6B. P2. (K1. P1) 3 times. P2. Rep from * to last **0** (**0-8-8-0-8**) sts. (C6B) **0** (**0-1-1-0-1**) time. P**0** (**0-2-2-0-2**).

14th row: K**0** (**0-2-2-0-2**). P**0** (**0-6-6-0-6**). K2. *(P1. K1) 3 times. K2. P6. K2. Rep from * to end of row.

15th row: P2. *K6. P2. (K1. P1) 3 times. P2. Rep from * to last **0** (**0-8-8-0-8**) sts. K**0** (**0-6-6-0-6**). P**0** (**0-2-2-0-2**).

16th to 23rd rows: As 14th and 15th rows 4 times more.

24th row: As 14th row.

Rep 1st to 24th rows for pat, AT SAME TIME, dec 1 st at beg of needle on next and every following 6th row to **28** (**30-40-36-48-56**) sts, then every following 4th row to **26** (**26-32-34-39-49**) sts.

Cont even in pat until work from beg measures **19** (**19**-**20**-**20**-**20**-**19**)" [**48** (**48**-**51**-**51**-**51**-**48**) cm], ending with a WS row.

Shape front placket: 1st row: (RS). Cast off 11 sts. Pat to end of row. **15** (**17**-**21**-**23**-**28**-**38**) sts.
Work 1 row even.

Shape neck edge and sleeve: Cont in pat, proceed as follows:
1st row: (RS). Pat to last 2 sts. Inc 1 st in next st. K1.
2nd row: Inc 1 st in first st. Pat to end of row.
Rep last 2 rows once more. **19** (**21**-**25**-**27**-**32**-**42**) sts.

Proceed as follows:
1st row: (RS). Pat to last 2 sts. Inc 1 st in next st. K1.
2nd row: Work even in pat.
Rep last 2 rows twice more, then rep 1st row once. **23** (**25**-**29**-**31**-**36**-**46**) sts.

Next row: (WS). Cast on **10** (**12**-**12**-**12**-**12**-**8**) sts. Pat to end of row. **33** (**37**-**41**-**43**-**48**-**54**) sts.
Work 2 rows even in pat. Place marker at end of last row.

Next row: (RS). K1. Work 2tog. Pat to end of row.
Work **17** (**0**-**11**-**0**-**7**-**3**) rows even.
Rep last **18** (**0**-**12**-**0**-**8**-**4**) rows **1** (**0**-**2**-**0**-**3**-**7**) time(s) more. **31** (**36**-**38**-**42**-**44**-**46**) sts.

Shape shoulder: Cast off **15** (**18**-**19**-**21**-**22**-**23**) sts beg of next row. Work 1 row even. Cast off rem **16** (**18**-**19**-**21**-**22**-**23**) sts.

FINISHING

Pin garment pieces to measurements. Cover with a damp cloth, leaving cloth to dry.

Sleeve bands: Sew shoulder seams. With RS facing and circular needle, pick up and knit **63** (**69**-**69**-**75**-**81**-**81**) sts across side edge between markers.
1st row: (RS). K3. *P3. K3. Rep from * to end of row.
2nd row: P3. *K3. P3. Rep from * to end of row.
Rep last 2 rows of (K3. P3) ribbing for 5" [12.5 cm], ending on a 2nd row. Cast off in rib.

Collar and placket edging: With RS facing and circular needle, pick up and knit **38** (**41**-**41**-**44**-**44**-**46**) sts up right front neck edge. K**24** (**24**-**24**-**28**-**28**-**28**) from back st holder, dec **1** (**1**-**1**-**1**-**1**-**3**) st(s) evenly across. Pick up and knit **38** (**41**-**41**-**44**-**44**-**46**) sts down left front neck edge. **99** (**105**-**105**-**115**-**115**-**117**) sts.
Work in (K3. P3) ribbing as given for Sleeve Bands until work measures same length as cast off edge of front placket, ending on a 2nd row. Leave sts on a spare needle.
Sew side edges of Collar and cast off edges of fronts tog.

Front edging: With RS facing and circular needle, pick up and knit **54** (**54**-**60**-**60**-**60**-**54**) sts up right front edge. Rib **99** (**105**-**105**-**115**-**115**-**117**) sts from spare needle. Pick up and knit **54** (**54**-**60**-**60**-**60**-**54**) sts down left front edge. **207** (**213**-**225**-**235**-**235**-**225**) sts.

Next row: Work in (K3. P3) ribbing.

Next row: Rib **52** (**52**-**58**-**58**-**52**-**52**) sts. Cast off 2 sts. Rib to end of row.

Next row: Work in (K3. P3) ribbing, casting on 2 sts over cast off sts.

Work 4 rows more in (K3. P3) ribbing. Cast off in rib.

BERET

With set of 4 smaller double-pointed needles, cast on 44 sts. Divide sts on needles as (14, 14, 16).

Join in rnd, placing marker at first st.

1st rnd: *K2. P2. Rep from * around.

Rep last rnd of (K2. P2) ribbing for 1½" [4 cm] .

Next rnd: *K2. M1. P2. M1. Rep from * to last 4 sts. K2. P2. 64 sts.

Change to larger needles and proceed in pat as follows:

1st rnd: *P2. C6B. P2. (K1. P1) 3 times. Rep from * around.

2nd rnd: *P2. K6. P2. (P1. K1) 3 times. Rep from * around.

3rd rnd: *P2. K6. P2. (K1. P1) 3 times. Rep from * around.

4th to 9th rnds: As 2nd and 3rd rnds 3 times more.

10th rnd: As 2nd rnd.

11th rnd: *P2. (P1. K1) 3 times. P2. C6B. Rep from * around.

12th rnd: *P2. (K1. P1) 3 times. P2. K6. Rep from * around.

13th rnd: *P2. (P1. K1) 3 times. P2. K6. Rep from * around.

14th to 19th rnds: As 12th and 13th rnds 3 times more.

20th rnd: As 12th rnd.

21st to 29th rnds: As 1st to 9th rnds once more.

Shape top: 1st rnd: *P2. ssk. K2. K2tog. P2. (P1. K1) 3 times. Rep from * around. 56 sts.

2nd rnd: *P2. (P1. K1) twice. P2. C6B. Rep from * around.

3rd rnd: *P2. (K1. P1) twice. P2. K6. Rep from * around.

4th rnd: *P2. (P1. K1) twice. P2. ssk. K2. K2tog. Rep from * around. 48 sts.

5th rnd: *P2. (K1. P1) twice. P2. K4. Rep from * around.

6th rnd: *P2. (P1. K1) twice. P2. K4. Rep from * around.

7th rnd: *P2tog. (K1. P1) twice. P2tog. K4. Rep from * around. 40 sts.

8th rnd: *P1. (P1. K1) twice. P1. K4. Rep from * around.

9th rnd: *P1. (K1. P1) twice. P1. K4. Rep from * around.

10th rnd: *P2. K1. P2tog. P1. K2. K2tog. Rep from * around. 32 sts.

11th rnd: *(P1. K1) twice. P1. K3. Rep from * around.

12th rnd: *C4B. (P1. K1) twice. Rep from * around.

13th rnd: *ssk. K2. P2tog. K1. P1. Rep from * around. 24 sts.

14th rnd: *K4. P1. K1. Rep from * around.

15th rnd: *K3. P1. K1. P1. Rep from * around.

16th rnd: *ssk. K1. P2tog. K1. Rep from * around. 18 sts.

17th rnd: *K2tog. Rep from * around. 9 sts. Break yarn leaving a long tail. Draw tail through rem sts and fasten securely. BERNAT

Chart I

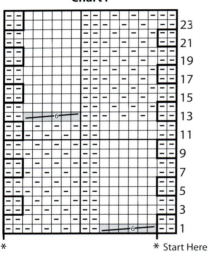

23
21
19
17
15
13
11
9
7
5
3
1

*   * Start Here

Key

☐ = Knit on RS rows. Purl on WS rows.

⊟ = Purl on RS rows. Knit on WS rows.

⊏━━6━━⊐ = C6B

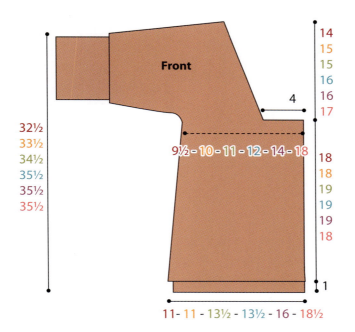

Front

4

14
15
15
16
16
17

9½ – 10 – 11 – 12 – 14 – 18

32½
33½
34½
35½
35½
35½

18
18
19
19
19
18

1

11 – 11 – 13½ – 13½ – 16 – 18½

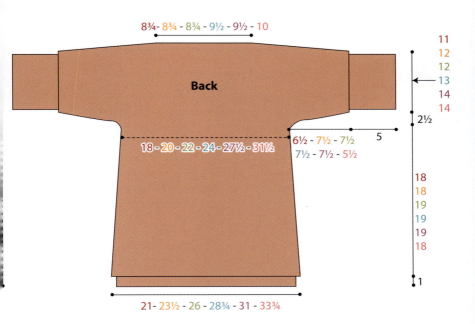

8¾ – 8¾ – 8¾ – 9½ – 9½ – 10

Back

11
12
12
13
14
14

2½

18 – 20 – 22 – 24 – 27½ – 31½

6½ – 7½ – 7½
7½ – 7½ – 5½

5

18
18
19
19
19
18

1

21 – 23½ – 26 – 28¾ – 31 – 33¾

2. Quick and Cozy Set

SUPER BULKY **EASY**

MEASUREMENTS

Mittens: One size to fit average lady.
Scarf: Approx 6" x 60" [15 x 152.5 cm]

GAUGES

Scarf: 10½ sts and 13 rows = 4" [10 cm] with larger needles in Seed St Pat.
Mittens: 13 sts and 16 rows = 4" [10 cm] with smaller needles in Seed St Pat.

MATERIALS

Bernat® Softee® Chunky™ (Ombres: 80 g/2.8/ oz; 70 m/77 yds)		
	Scarf: 29521 (Native Ombre)	**3 balls**
Size 8 mm (U.S. 11) knitting needles **or size needed to obtain gauge.**		
	Mittens: 29521 (Native Ombre)	**2 balls**
Size 6.5 mm (U.S. 10½) knitting needles **or size needed to obtain gauge.**		

ABBREVIATIONS
See page 65 for Helpful Hints.

Alt = Alternate(ing).
Approx = Approximately.
Beg = Begin(ning).
Cont = Continue(ity).

K = Knit.
K2(3)tog = Knit next 2 (3) stitches together.
P = Purl.
P2(3)tog = Purl next 2(3) stitches together.

Pat = Pattern.
Rem = Remain(ing).
Rep = Repeat.
RS = Right side.
St(s) = Stitch(es).
WS = Wrong side.

INSTRUCTIONS

SCARF

With larger needles, cast on 15 sts.

1st row: (RS). *K1. P1. Rep from * to last st. K1.

Rep last row for Seed St Pat until work from beg measures 60" [152.5 cm] , ending with a RS row.

Cast off in pat.

Pom-pom: (make 2). Wind yarn around 4 fingers approx 100 times. Remove from fingers and tie tightly in center. Cut through each side of loops. Trim to a smooth round shape. Gather ends of Scarf and sew a pom-pom to each end.

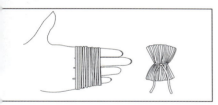

MITTENS

Right Mitten

****With smaller needles, cast on 23 sts.

1st row: (RS). *K1. P1. Rep from * to last st. K1.

2nd row: *P1. K1. Rep from * to last st. P1.

Rep last 2 rows of (K1. P1) ribbing for 3" [7.5 cm], ending with a WS row.

Proceed in pat as follows:

1st row: (RS). *K1. P1. Rep from * to last st. K1.

Rep last row for Seed St Pat 5 times more.**

Shape thumb gusset: 1st row: (RS). Pat across 12 sts. (K1. P1. K1) all in next st. Pat to end of row. 25 sts.

Work 5 rows even in pat.

Next row: Pat across 12 sts. (K1. P1. K1) all in next st. P1. (K1. P1. K1) all in next st. Pat to end of row. 29 sts.

Work 5 rows even in pat.

Shape thumb: Next row: (RS). Pat across 19 sts. **Turn.** Leave rem sts on a spare needle.

*****Next row:** Cast on 1 st. Pat across 8 sts (including cast on st). **Turn.** Leave rem sts on a spare needle.

Next row: Cast on 1 st. Pat across 9 sts (including cast on st).

Work 5 rows even in pat on these 9 sts.

Next row: (RS). (P1. K3tog) twice. P1. 5 sts.

Next row: (P2tog) twice. P1. 3 sts.

Break yarn, leaving a long end. Draw end tightly through rem sts. Sew thumb seam.

Next row: (RS). Rejoin yarn at thumb opening. Pick up and knit 2 sts over cast on sts at base of thumb. Pat to end of row.

Next row: Pat across to 2 picked up sts. K2tog (picked up sts). Pat to end of row. 23 sts.

Cont in pat until work after ribbing measures 6½" [16.5 cm], ending with a WS row.

Shape top: 1st row: (RS). K1. P3tog. Pat across next 8 sts. K3tog. Pat to end of row. 19 sts.

2nd and alt rows: Work even in pat.

3rd row: K1. P3tog. Pat across next 6 sts. K3tog. Pat to end of row. 15 sts.

5th row: K1. P3tog. Pat across next 4 sts. K3tog. Pat to end of row. 11 sts.

7th row: K1. P3tog. Pat across next 2 sts. K3tog. Pat to end of row. 7 sts.

Break yarn, leaving a long end. Draw end tightly through rem sts. Sew side seam.***

Left Mitten

Work from ** to ** as given for Right Mitten.

Shape thumb gusset: 1st row: (RS). Pa across 8 sts. (K1. P1. K1) all in next st. Pat to end of row. 25 sts.

Work 5 rows even in pat.

Next row: Pat across 8 sts. (K1. P1. K1) all in next st. P1. (K1. P1. K1) all in next st. Pat to end of row. 29 sts.

Work 5 rows even in pat.

Shape Thumb: Next row: (RS). Pat acros 15 sts. **Turn.** Leave rem sts on a spare needle.

Work from *** to *** as given for Right Mitten. **BERNAT**

3. Unisex Classic Set

	JACKET: ■ ■ □ ▷
✂ ///// 🥄 ⑥	EASY
DOUBLE-POINTED CIRCULAR SUPER	HAT: ■ □ □ ▷
NEEDLES NEEDLE BULKY	BEGINNER

SIZES

Jacket

To fit bust/chest measurement
Extra-Small/Small 28-34" [71-86.5 cm]
Medium 36-38" [91.5-96.5 cm]
Large 40-42" [101.5-106.5 cm]
Extra-Large 44-46" [112-117 cm]
2/3 Extra-Large 48-54" [122-137 cm]
4/5 Extra-Large 56-62" [142-157.5 cm]

Finished bust/chest		
Extra-Small/Small:	36"	[91.5 cm]
Medium:	40"	[101.5 cm]
Large:	44"	[112 cm]
Extra-Large:	48"	[122 cm]
2/3 Extra-Large:	54½"	[138.5 cm]
4/5 Extra-Large:	63"	[160 cm]

Hat: To fit average **Lady's** (**Man's**) head.

GAUGES

Jacket: 11 sts and 14 rows = 4" [10 cm] with larger needles in stocking st.

Hat: 9½ sts and 17 rows = 4" [10 cm] in garter st.

MATERIALS

Bernat® Softee® Chunky™ (100 g/3.5 oz; 99 m/108 yds)								
Jacket	**Sizes**	**XS/S**	**M**	**L**	**XL**	**2/3XL**	**4/5XL**	
28041 (Clay)	**Her Version**	7	8	9	10	11	12	**balls**
	His Version	8	9	10	11	12	13	**balls**

Sizes 6.5 mm (U.S. 10½) and 8 mm (U.S. 11) knitting needles. Size 6.5 mm (U.S. 10½) circular knitting needle 24" [60 cm] long **or size needed to obtain gauge.** Set of four sizes 6.5 mm (U.S. 10½) and 8 mm (U.S. 11) double-pointed knitting needles. Separating zipper approx **20** (**20-22-22-22-23½**)" [**50** (**50-55-55-55-60**) cm] long for Her Version or **22** (**22-23½-23½-25½-25½**)" [**55** (**55-60-60-65-65**) cm] long for His Version. 2 st holders.

Hat	**Sizes**	**Lady**	**Man**	
28041 (Clay)		1	1	**ball**

Size 9 mm (U.S. 13) knitting needles **or size needed to obtain gauge.**

ABBREVIATIONS

See page 65 for Helpful Hints.

Alt = Alternate(ing).
Approx = Approximately.
Beg = Beginning.
Cont = Continue(ity).
Inc = Increase 1 stitch by knitting into front and back of next stitch.
K = Knit.
K2tog = Knit next 2 stitches together.
P = Purl.
P2tog = Purl next 2 stitches together.
P2togtbl = Purl next 2 stitches together through back loops.
Pat = Pattern.
Rem = Remaining.
Rep = Repeat.
Rnd(s) = Round(s).
RS = Right side.
Sl1 = Slip next stitch knitwise.
Ssk = Slip next 2 stitches knitwise one at a time. Pass them back onto left-hand needle, then knit through back loops together
St(s) = Stitch(es).
Tog = Together.
WS = Wrong Side.

INSTRUCTIONS

JACKET

The instructions are written for smallest size. If changes are necessary for larger sizes the instructions will be written thus ( ). Numbers for each size are shown in the same color throughout the pattern. When only one number is given in black, it applies to all sizes.

Note: Body is worked in one piece to armholes.

BODY

**With smaller circular needle, cast on 98 (110-118-130-150-174) sts. Do not join. Working back and forth across needle in rows, proceed as follows:

1st row: (RS). *K2. P2. Rep from * to last 2 sts. K2.

2nd row: *P2. K2. Rep from * to last 2 sts. P2.

Rep last 2 rows (K2. P2) ribbing for 2½" [6 cm], ending on a 2nd row and inc **2** (**0**-**2**-**2**-**2**-**0**) sts evenly across last row. **100** (**110**-**120**-**132**-**150**-**174**) sts.

Change to larger circular needle and work in stocking st until work from beg measures 16" [40.5 cm] for Lady's Version or 18" [45.5 cm] for Man's Version, ending with a purl row.

Divide for armholes: Next row: (RS). K**23** (**26**-**27**-**29**-**34**-**40**). Cast off next **4** (**4**-**4**-**6**-**8**-**8**) sts. Pat **46** (**50**-**54**-**58**-**66**-**78**) (including st on needle after cast off). Cast off next **4** (**4**-**4**-**6**-**8**-**8**) sts. K**23** (**26**-**27**-**29**-**34**-**40**). (including st on needle after cast off).

Left Front: Cont on last **23** (**26**-**27**-**29**-**34**-**40**) sts as follows:

Sizes XS/S, M, L, XL and 2/3XL only: 1st row: (WS). Purl.
2nd row: K1. ssk. Knit to end of row.
Rep last 2 rows **5** (**6**-**8**-**9**-**9**) times more. **17** (**19**-**18**-**19**-**24**) sts.

Sizes M and XL only: Shape neck: 1st row: (RS). K1. ssk. Knit to end of row.
2nd row: P3. Slip these 3 sts onto a st holder. Purl to end of row. 15 sts rem.
3rd row: K1. ssk. Knit to last 3 sts. K2tog. K1.
4th row: P1. P2tog. Purl to end of row. 12 sts rem.

Sizes XS/S and L only: Shape neck: 1st row: (RS). K1. ssk. Knit to end of row.
2nd row: P**2** (**3**) sts. Slip these **2** (**3**) sts on a st holder. Purl to end of row. 14 sts rem.

Sizes XS/S, M, L and XL only: Next row: K1. ssk. Knit to last 3 sts. K2tog. K1.
Next row: Purl.
Rep last 2 rows **1** (**0**-**1**-**0**) time more. 10 sts rem.

Next row: (RS). K1. ssk. Knit to last 3 sts. K2tog. K1.
Next row: Purl.
Rep last 2 rows once more. 6 sts rem.

Next row: (RS). K1. ssk. K2tog. K1.
Next row: Purl.
Next row: ssk. K2tog.
Next row: Purl.
Next row: ssk. Fasten off.

Size 2/3XL only: Shape neck: 1st row: (RS). K1. ssk. Knit to end of row.
2nd row: P3. Slip these 3 sts onto a st holder. Purl to last 3 sts. P2togtbl. P1. 19 sts rem.
3rd row: K1. ssk. Knit to last 3 sts. K2tog. K1.
4th row: Purl.
5th row: As 3rd row.
6th row: Purl to last 3 sts P2togtbl. P1.
Rep last 4 rows once more. 9 sts rem.

Size 4/5XL only: 1st row: (WS). Purl.
2nd row: K1. ssk. Knit to end of row.
Rep last 2 rows once more, then 1st row once. 38 sts.

Proceed as follows:

1st row: K1. ssk. Knit to end of row.

2nd row: Purl to last 3 sts. P2tog. P1.

3rd row: As 1st row.

4th row: Purl.

Rep last 4 rows 3 times more. 26 sts rem.

Shape neck: 1st row: (RS). K1. ssk. Knit to end of row.

2nd row: P3. Slip these 3 sts onto a st holder. Purl to last 3 sts. P2togtbl. P1.

3rd row: K1. ssk. Knit to last 3 sts. K2tog. K1.

4th row: P1. P2tog. Purl to end of row.

5th row: As 3rd row.

6th row: P1. P2tog. Purl to last 3 sts P2togtbl. P1.

7th row: K1. ssk. Knit to last 3 sts. K2tog. K1.

8th row: Purl.

9th row: As 3rd row.

10th row: Purl to last 3 sts. P2togtbl. P1. 9 sts rem.

Sizes 2/3XL and 4/5XL only: 1st row: K1. ssk. K3. K2tog. K1.

2nd row: P4. P2togtbl. P1.

3rd row: K1. ssk. K2tog. K1.

4th row: P4.

5th row: ssk. K2tog.

6th row: P2.

7th row: ssk. Fasten off.

Back: With WS facing, rejoin yarn to **46** (**50**-**54**-**58**-**66**-**78**) sts for Back.

Sizes XS/S, M, L, XL and 2/3XL only: 1st row: (WS). Purl.

2nd row: K1. ssk. Pat to last 3 sts. K2tog. K1. Rep last 2 rows **13** (**14**-**16**-**17**-**10**) times more. **18** (**20**-**20**-**22**-**44**) sts rem.

Size 4/5XL only: 1st row: (WS). Purl.

2nd row: K1. ssk. Pat to last 3 sts. K2tog. K1. Rep last 2 rows twice more, then 1st row once. **70** sts.

Sizes 2/3XL and 4/5XL only: 1st row: (RS). K1. ssk. Knit to last 3 sts. K2tog. K1.

2nd row: P1. P2togtbl. Purl to last 3 sts. P2togtbl. P1.

3rd row: As 1st row.

4th row: Purl.

Rep last 4 rows (**3**-**7**) times more. (**20**-**22**) sts rem.

All sizes: Cast off.

Right Front: With WS facing, rejoin yarn to rem **23** (**26**-**27**-**29**-**34**-**40**) sts.

Sizes XS/S, M, L, XL and 2/3XL only: 1st row: (WS). Purl.

2nd row: Knit to last 3 sts. K2tog. K1. Rep last 2 rows **5** (**6**-**8**-**9**-**9**) times more. **17** (**19**-**18**-**19**-**24**) sts.

M and XL only: Shape neck: 1st row: (RS). K3. Slip these 3 sts onto a st holder. Knit to last 3 sts. K2tog. K1. 15 sts rem.

2nd row: Purl.

3rd row: K1. ssk. Knit to last 3 sts. K2tog. K1.

4th row: Purl to last 3 sts. P2tog. P1. 12 sts rem.

Sizes XS/S and L only: Shape neck:
1st row: (RS). K2 (3) sts. Slip these 2 (3) sts onto a st holder. Knit to last 3 sts. K2tog. K1. 14 sts rem.
2nd row: Purl.
Sizes XS/S, M, L and XL only: Next row: K1. ssk. Knit to last 3 sts. K2tog. K1.
Next row: Purl.
Rep last 2 rows 1 (0-1-0) time more. 10 sts rem.

Next row: (RS). K1. ssk. Knit to last 3 sts. K2tog. K1.
Next row: Purl.
Rep last 2 rows once more. 6 sts rem.

Next row: (RS). K1. ssk. K2tog. K1.
Next row: Purl.
Next row: ssk. K2tog.
Next row: Purl.
Next row: K2tog. Fasten off.

Size 2/3XL only: Shape neck: 1st row: (RS). K3. Slip these 3 sts onto a st holder. Knit to last 3 sts. K2tog. K1.
2nd row: P1. P2tog. Purl to end of row. 19 sts rem.
3rd row: K1. ssk. Knit to last 3 sts. K2tog. K1.
4th row: Purl.
5th row: As 3rd row.
6th row: P1. P2tog. Purl to end of row.
Rep last 4 rows once more. 9 sts rem.

Size 4/5XL only: 1st row: (WS). Purl.
2nd row: Knit to last 3 sts. K2tog. K1.
Rep last 2 rows once more, then 1st row once. 38 sts.

Proceed as follows:
1st row: Knit to last 3 sts. K2tog. K1.
2nd row: P1. P2tog. Purl to end of row.
3rd row: As 1st row.
4th row: Purl.
Rep last 4 rows 3 times more. 26 sts rem.

Shape neck: 1st row: (RS). K3. Slip these 3 sts onto a st holder. Knit to last 3 sts. K2tog. K1.
2nd row: P1. P2tog. Purl to end of row.
3rd row: K1. ssk. Knit to last 3 sts. K2tog. K1.
4th row: Purl to last 3 sts. P2tog. P1.
5th row: As 3rd row.
6th row: P1. P2tog. Purl to last 3 sts. P2togtbl. P1.
7th row: K1. ssk. Knit to last 3 sts. K2tog. K1.
8th row: Purl.
9th row: As 3rd row.
10th row: P1. P2tog. Purl to end of row. 9 sts rem.

Sizes 2/3XL and 4/5XL only: 1st row: K1. ssk. K3. K2tog. K1.
2nd row: P1. P2togtbl. P4.
3rd row: K1. ssk. K2tog. K1.
4th row: P4.
5th row: ssk. K2tog.
6th row: P2.
7th row: K2tog. Fasten off.

SLEEVES

With smaller set of 4 needles, cast on 28 sts. Divide sts onto 3 needles (8, 8, 12) sts.

1st rnd: *K2. P2. Rep from * around.

Rep last rnd of (K2. P2) ribbing for 2½" [6 cm], inc 2 sts evenly around. 30 sts.

Change to larger set of needles and knit in rnds, inc 1 st at beg and end of **11th** (**7th-5th**-**5th**-**5th**-**5th**) rnd and every following **10th** (**8th**-**6th**-**6th**-**6th**-**4th**) rnd until there are **38** (**34**-**38**-**46**-**36**-**54**) sts.

Sizes M, L, 2/3XL only: Inc 1 st each at beg and end of every following (**8th**-**6th**-**6th**) rnd from previous inc until there are (**40**-**44**-**50**) sts.

All sizes: Knit even until work from beg measures **17½** (**17½**-**18**-**18**-**17**-**16½**)" [**44.5** (**44.5**-**45.5**-**45.5**-**44.5**-**42**) cm] for Lady's Version or 18½" [47 cm] for Man's Version.

Shape raglans: Next rnd: Cast off **2** (**3**-**3**-**4**-**4**-**4**) sts. K**34** (**34**-**38**-**38**-**42**-**46**). Cast off rem **2** (**3**-**3**-**4**-**4**-**4**) sts.

Re-join yarn to rem **34** (**34**-**38**-**38**-**42**-**46**) sts and cont working back and forth across needle in rows as follows:

1st row: (RS). K1. ssk. Knit to last 3 sts. K2tog. K1.

2nd row: Purl.

Rep last 2 rows **10** (**11**-**15**-**16**-**17**-**13**) times more. **12** (**10**-**6**-**4**-**6**-**18**) sts rem.

Sizes XS/S, M and 4/5XL only: 1st row: (RS). K1. ssk. Knit to last 3 sts. K2tog. K1.

2nd row: P1. P2tog. Purl to last 3 sts. P2togtbl. P1.

3rd row: As 1st row.

4th row: Purl.

Rep last 4 rows **0** (**0**-**1**) time more. **6** (**4**-**6**) sts rem.

All sizes: Cast off.

FINISHING

Pin all pieces to measurements. Cover with a damp cloth, leaving cloth to dry.
Sew raglan seams.

Right Shawl Collar: With **WS** facing and smaller needles, K**2** (**3**-**3**-**3**-**3**-**3**) from right front st holder.

1st row: (RS). Sl1. Inc 1 st in next st. Knit to end of row.

2nd and alt rows: Knit.

3rd row: Sl1. Inc 1 st in next st. Knit to end of row.

5th row: Sl1. Knit to last 2 sts. Inc 1 st in next st. Knit to end of row.

6th row: Knit.

Rep last 2 rows until there are 20 sts.

Cont even in garter st (knit every row) until Collar measures length to fit to center of Back, ending with a RS row. Break yarn. Leave sts on a spare needle.

Left Shawl Collar: With RS facing and smaller needles, K**2** (**3**-**3**-**3**-**3**-**3**) from left front st holder.

1st row: (WS). Sl1. Knit to end of row.
2nd row: Inc 1 st in first st. Knit to end of row.
3rd row: Sl1. Knit to end of row.
4th row: Inc 1 st in first st. Knit to end of row. Rep last 2 rows until there are 20 sts.

Cont even in garter st until Collar measures length to fit to center of Back, ending with a WS row. **Do not b**reak yarn.

3 needle cast off: Align 2 needles with Right and Left Collars facing RS tog. Knit first stitch from each needle tog. *Knit next stitch from each needle tog. Pass first st on right-hand needle over second st. Rep from * until all sts will be cast off.

Zipper edging: With RS facing and smaller needle, pick up and knit **53** (**55**-**57**-**59**-**59**-**60**) sts for Her Version or **59** (**60**-**63**-**65**-**65**-**66**) sts for His Version up Right Front to beg of neck shaping. Cast off.
Rep for Left Front. Sew zipper in position, folding extra length at neck edge.

HAT

The instructions are written for Lady's size. If changes are necessary for Man's size the instructions will be written thus ( ). Numbers for each size are shown in the same color throughout the pattern. When only one number is given in black, it applies to both sizes.

Cast on **46** (**50**) sts.
Work in garter st (knit every row) until work from beg measures **5** (**5½**)" [**12.5** (**14**) cm] noting first row is RS and ending on a WS row.

Shape top: 1st row: (RS). K1. *K2tog. K**7** (**8**). ssk. Rep from * to last st. K1. **38** (**42**) sts.
2nd to 4th rows: Knit.
5th row: K1. *K2tog. K**5** (**6**). ssk. Rep from * to last st. K1. **30** (**34**) sts.
6th to 8th rows: Knit.
9th row: K1. *K2tog. K**3** (**4**). ssk. Rep from * to last st. K1. **22** (**26**) sts.
10th row: Knit.
11th row: K1. *K2tog. K**1** (**2**). ssk. Rep from * to last st. K1. **14** (**18**) sts.
12th row: Knit.
13th row: *K2tog. Rep from * to end of row. **7** (**9**) sts.

Break yarn leaving a long end. Draw end through rem sts and fasten securely.
Sew center back seam.

Optional: Pom-pom: Wind yarn around 4 fingers approx 60 times. Remove from fingers and tie tightly in center. Cut through each side of loops. Trim to a smooth round shape. Sew pom-pom to top of Hat. **BERNAT**

Sewing Garter Edges

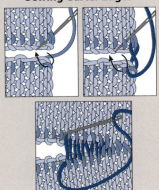

Thread yarn end through blunt ended large eye needle. Working with the right side facing, insert needle into first ridge at bottom of work. Draw needle through ridge on opposite side of seam. Continue drawing needle through alternating ridges at each side of seam.

After you have joined a few rows, pull the yarn, but not too tightly, to merge the 2 sides together (tog).

Continue the process to the end of seam. Cut the yarn leaving a 6" [15 cm] end. Weave the end into seam.

Pom-pom

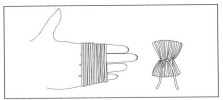

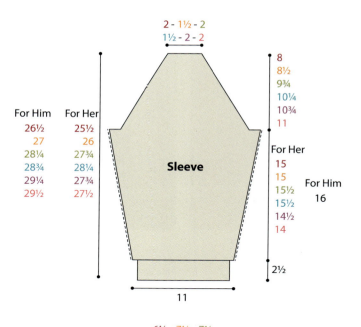

2 - 1½ - 2
1½ - 2 - 2

8
8½
9¾
10¼
10¾
11

For Her
15
15
15½
15½
14½
14

For Him
16

For Him   For Her
26½   25½
27   26
28¼   27¾
28¾   28¼
29¼   27¾
29½   27½

Sleeve

2½

11

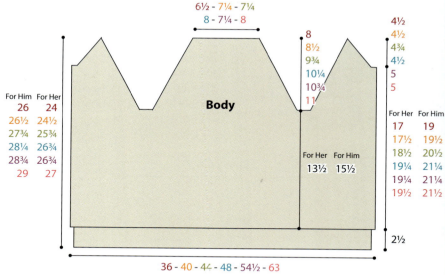

6½ - 7¼ - 7¼
8 - 7¼ - 8

4½
4½
4¾
4½
5
5

8
8½
9¾
10¼
10¾
11

For Him   For Her
26   24
26½   24½
27¾   25¾
28¼   26¾
28¾   26¾
29   27

Body

For Her   For Him
17   19
17½   19½
18½   20½
19¼   21¼
19¼   21¼
19½   21½

For Her   For Him
13½   15½

2½

36 - 40 - 44 - 48 - 54½ - 63

Knitting Needle Conversion Chart

Canadian & U.K. Sizes	–	–	000	00	0	1	2	3	4	5	6	7	8	9	–	10	11	12	13	14	15
Metric Sizes (mm)	15	12.75	10	9	8	7.5	7	6.5	6	5.5	5	4.5	4	3.75	3.5	3.25	2.75	2.5	2.25	2	1.75
U.S. Sizes	19	17	15	13	11	–	–	10½	10	9	8	7	6	5	4	3	–	2	1	0	–

4. Aran Cables Set

CIRCULAR NEEDLE SUPER BULKY INTERMEDIATE

SIZES
Cardigan

To fit bust measurement
Extra-Small/Small 28-34" [71-86.5 cm]
Medium 36-38" [91.5-96.5 cm]
Large 40-42" [101.5-106.5 cm]
Extra-Large 44-46" [112-117 cm]
2/3 Extra-Large 48-54" [122-137 cm]
4/5 Extra-Large 56-62" [142-157.5 cm]

Finished bust	
Extra-Small/Small:	37" [94 cm]
Medium:	40" [101.5 cm]
Large:	44" [112 cm]
Extra-Large:	48" [122 cm]
2/3 Extra-Large:	54" [137 cm]
4/5 Extra-Large:	60" [152.5 cm]

Hat: One size to fit average lady's head.

GAUGE
11 sts and 14 rows = 4" [10 cm] with larger needles in stocking st.

MATERIALS

Bernat® Softee® Chunky™ (100 g/3.5 oz; 99 m/108 yds)

Cardigan	Sizes	XS/S	M	L	XL	2/3XL	4/5XL	
28021 (Linen)		9	10	11	12	13	14	**balls**

Sizes 6.5 mm (U.S. 10½) and 8 mm (U.S. 11) knitting needles. Size 6.5 mm (U.S. 10½) circular knitting needle 24" [60 cm] long **or size needed to obtain gauge.** Cable needle. 3 st holders. 5 buttons.

Hat

 28021 (Linen)   **1 ball**

Sizes 6.5 mm (U.S. 10½) and 8 mm (U.S. 11) knitting needles **or size needed to obtain gauge.** Cable needle.

ABBREVIATIONS

See page 65 for Helpful Hints.

2tog = K2tog or P2tog.

Approx = Approximately.

Alt = Alternate(ing).

Beg = Beginning.

Cr4F = Slip next stitch onto cable needle and leave at front of work. K3, then K1 from cable needle.

Cr4B = Slip next 3 stitches onto cable needle and leave at back of work. K1, then K3 from cable needle.

Cont = Continue(ity).

Dec = Decrease(ing).

Inc = Increase.

K = Knit.

K1tbl = Knit next stitch through back of loop.

K2tog = Knit next 2 stitches together.

P = Purl.

P1tbl = Purl next stitch through back of loop.

P2tog = Purl next 2 stitches together.

P2togtbl = Purl next 2 stitches together through back loops.

Pat = Pattern.

Psso = Pass slipped stitch over.

Rem = Remain(ing).

Rep = Repeat.

RS = Right side.

Sl1 = Slip next stitch.

Ssk = Slip next 2 stitches knitwise one at a time. Pass them back onto left-hand needle, then knit through back loops together.

St(s) = Stitch(es).

T2F = Slip next stitch onto cable needle and leave at front of work. P1, then K1tbl from cable needle.

T2B = Slip next stitch onto cable needle and leave at back of work. K1tbl, then P1 from cable needle.

T3F = Slip next stitch onto cable needle and leave at front of work. K1tbl, P1, then K1tbl from cable needle.

WS = Wrong side.

Yo = Yarn over.

INSTRUCTIONS

CARDIGAN

The instructions are written for smallest size. If changes are necessary for larger sizes the instructions will be written thus ( ). Numbers for each size are shown in the same color throughout the pattern. When only one number is given in black, it applies to all sizes.

CABLE PANEL A (worked over 13 sts).
(See Chart II on page 36).
1st row: (RS). P5. T3F. P5.
2nd row: K5. P1tbl. K1. P1tbl. K5.
3rd row: P4. T2B. K1. T2F. P4.
4th row: K4. P1tbl. K1. P1. K1. P1tbl. K4.
5th row: P3. T2B. K1. P1. K1. T2F. P3.
6th row: K3. P1tbl. (K1. P1) twice. K1. P1tbl. K3.
7th row: P2. T2B. (K1. P1) twice. K1. T2F. P2.
8th row: K2. P1tbl. (K1. P1) 3 times. K1. P1tbl. K2.
9th row: P1. T2B. (K1. P1) 3 times. K1. T2F. P1.
10th row: K1. P1tbl. (K1. P1) 4 times. K1. P1tbl. K1.
11th row: P1. T2F. (P1. K1) 3 times. P1. T2B. P1.
12th row: As 8th row.
13th row: P2. T2F. (P1. K1) twice. P1. T2B. P2.
14th row: As 6th row.
15th row: P3. T2F. P1. K1. P1. T2B. P3.
16th row: As 4th row.
17th row: P4. T2F. P1. T2B. P4.
18th row: As 2nd row.
These 18 rows form Cable Panel A.

CABLE PANEL B (worked over 11 sts).
(See Chart III on page 36).
1st row: (RS). P1. Cr4F. K1. Cr4B. P1.
2nd row: K1. P9. K1.
3rd row: P1. K9. P1.
4th row: As 2nd row.
These 4 rows form Cable Panel B.

BACK

With smaller needles, cast on **49** (**53-57-61-69-77**) sts.
1st row: (RS). *P1. K1tbl. Rep from * to last st. P1.
2nd row: *K1. P1tbl. Rep from * to last st. K1.
Rep last 2 rows Twisted Ribbing Pat for 4" [10 cm], ending on a 2nd row and inc 3 sts evenly across last row. **52** (**56-60-64-72-80**) sts.

Change to larger needles and proceed in pat as follows:
1st row: (RS). *K2. P2. Rep from * to end of row.
2nd row: *K2. P2. Rep from * to end of row.
3rd row: *P2. K2. Rep from * to end of row.
4th row: *P2. K2. Rep from * to end of row.
These 4 rows form Box St Pat.

Cont in Box St Pat until work from beg measures **17** (**17-16½-16½-16-16**)" [**43** (**43-42-42-40.5-40.5**) cm], ending with a WS row.

Shape raglans: Keeping cont of pat, cast off **2** (**2-2-3-3-3**) sts beg next 2 rows. **48** (**52-56-58-66-74**) sts rem.

Size XS/S only: 1st row: (RS). K2. ssk. Pat to last 4 sts. K2tog. K2.

2nd row: P3. Pat to last 3 sts. P3.

3rd row: K3. Pat to last 3 sts. K3.

4th row: As 2nd row.

Rep last 4 rows once more. 44 sts rem.

Sizes XL, 2/3XL and 4/5XL only: 1st row: (RS). K2. ssk. Pat to last 4 sts. K2tog. K2.

2nd row: P2. P2tog. Pat to last 4 sts. P2togtbl. P2.

3rd row: As 1st row.

4th row: P3. Pat to last 3 sts. P3.

Rep last 4 rows (0-3-6) times more. (52-42-32) sts rem.

All sizes: 1st row: K2. ssk. Pat to last 4 sts. K2tog. K2.

2nd row: P3. Pat to last 3 sts. P3.

Rep last 2 rows 11 (15-16-14-9-4) times more. 20 (20-22-22-22-22) sts rem.

LEFT FRONT

**With smaller needles, cast on 29 (31-33-35-41-47) sts.

Work 4" [10 cm] in Twisted Ribbing Pat as given for Back, ending on a 2nd row and inc 4 sts evenly across last row. 33 (35-37-39-45-51) sts.**

Change to larger needles and proceed in pat as follows:

1st row: (RS). K0 (2-0-2-0-2). (P2. K2) 1 (1-2-2-4-5) time(s). P2. K1tbl. Work 1st row Cable Panel B. K1tbl. Work 1st row Cable Panel A. P1.

2nd row: K1. Work 2nd row Cable Panel A. P1tbl. Work 2nd row Cable Panel B. P1tbl. K2 (P2. K2) 1 (1-2-2-4-5) time(s). P0 (2-0-2 0-2)

3rd row: P0 (2-0-2-0-2). (K2. P2) 1 (1-2-2-4-5) time(s). P2. K1tbl. Work 3rd row Cable Panel B. K1tbl. Work 3rd row Cable Panel A. P1.

4th row: K1. Work 4th row Cable Panel A. P1tbl. Work 4th row Cable Panel B. P1tbl. K2. (K2. P2) 1 (1-2-2-4-5) time(s). K0 (2-0-2-0-2).

Last 4 rows form Box St Pat at side. Cable Panel Pats A and B are now in position.

Cont even in pat until work from beg measures same length as Back to beg of raglan shaping, ending with a WS row.

Shape raglan: Keeping cont of pat, cast off 2 (2-2-3-3-3) sts beg next row. 31 (33-35-36-42-48) sts rem.

Next row: Pat to last 3 sts. P3.

Sizes XS/S, M and L only: Shape raglan and front: 1st row: K2. ssk. Pat to last 2 sts. Work 2tog.

2nd row: Pat to last 3 sts. P3.

Rep last 2 rows 10 (14-15) times more. 9 (3-3) sts rem.

Size XS/S only: 1st row: K2. ssk. Pat to end of row.

2nd row: Pat to last 3 sts. P3.

3rd row: K2. ssk. Pat to last 2 sts. Work 2tog.

4th row: As 2nd row.

5th row: As 1st row.

6th row: As 2nd row.

7th row: K1. ssk. Work 2tog.

8th row: P3. 3 sts rem.

Sizes XL, 2/3XL and 4/5XL only: Shape raglan and front: 1st row: K2. ssk. Pat to last 2 sts. Work 2tog.

2nd row: Pat to last 4 sts. P2togtbl. P2.

3rd row: As 1st row.

4th row: Pat to last 3 sts. P3.

Rep last 4 rows (**1**-**4**-**8**) time(s) more. (**26**-**17**-**3**) sts rem.

Sizes XL and 2/3XL only: 1st row: K2. ssk. Pat to last 2 sts. Work 2tog.

2nd row: Pat to last 3 sts. P3.

Rep last 2 rows (**9**-**6**) times more. (**6**-**3**) sts rem.

Size XL only: 1st row: K2. ssk. Pat to end of row.

2nd row: Pat to last 3 sts. P3.

3rd row: K1. ssk. Work 2tog.

4th row: P3. 3 sts rem.

All sizes: 1st row: K1. ssk.

2nd row: P2.

3rd row: ssk. Fasten off.

RIGHT FRONT

Work from ** to ** as given for Left Front. Change to larger needles and proceed in pat as follows:

1st row: (RS). P1. Work 1st row Cable Panel A. K1tbl. Work 1st row Cable Panel B. K1tbl. P2. (K2. P2) **1** (**1**-**2**-**2**-**4**-**5**) time(s). K**0** (**2**-**0**-**2**-**0**-**2**).

2nd row: P**0** (**2**-**0**-**2**-**0**-**2**). (K2. P2) **1** (**1**-**2**-**2**-**4**-**5**) time(s). K2. P1tbl. Work 2nd row Cable Panel B. P1tbl. Work 2nd row Cable Panel A. K1.

3rd row: P1. Work 3rd row Cable Panel A. K1tbl. Work 3rd row Cable Panel B. K1tbl. P2. (P2. K2) **1** (**1**-**2**-**2**-**4**-**5**) time(s). P**0** (**2**-**0**-**2**-**0**-**2**).

4th row: K**0** (**2**-**0**-**2**-**0**-**2**). (P2. K2) **1** (**1**-**2**-**2**-**4**-**5**) time(s). K2. P1tbl. Work 4th row Cable Panel B. P1tbl. Work 4th row Cable Panel A. K1.

Last 4 rows form Box St Pat at side. Cable Panel Pats A and B are now in position.

Cont even in pat until work from beg measures same length as Back to beg of raglan shaping, ending with a RS row.

Shape raglan: Keeping cont of pat, cast off **2** (**2**-**2**-**3**-**3**-**3**) sts beg next row. **31** (**33**-**35**-**36**-**42**-**48**) sts rem.

Sizes XS/S, M and L only: Shape raglan and front: 1st row: Work 2tog. Pat to last 4 sts. K2tog. K2.

2nd row: P3. Pat to end of row.

Rep last 2 rows **10** (**14**-**15**) times more. **9** (**3**-**3**) sts rem.

Size XS/S only: 1st row: Work 2tog. Pat to end of row.

2nd row: P3. Pat to end of row.

3rd row: Work 2tog. Pat to last 4 sts. K2tog. K2.

4th row: As 2nd row.

5th row: As 1st row.

6th row: As 2nd row.

7th row: Work 2tog. K2tog. K1.

8th row: P3. 3 sts rem.

Sizes XL, 2/3XL and 4/5XL only: Shape raglan and front: 1st row: Work 2tog. Pat to last 4 sts. K2tog. K2.

2nd row: P2. P2tog. Pat to end of row.

3rd row: As 1st row.

4th row: P3. Pat to end of row.

Rep last 4 rows (1-4-8) time(s) more. (26-17-3) sts rem.

Sizes XL and 2/3XL only: 1st row: Work 2tog. Pat to last 4 sts. K2tog. K2.

2nd row: P3. Pat to end of row.

Rep last 2 rows (9-6) times more. (6-3) sts rem.

Size XL only: 1st row: Pat to last 4 sts. K2tog. K2.

2nd row: P3. Pat to end of row.

3rd row: Work 2tog. K2tog. K1.

4th row: P3. 3 sts rem.

All sizes: 1st row: K2tog. K1.

2nd row: P2.

3rd row: K2tog. Fasten off.

SLEEVES

With smaller needles, cast on **29** (**29-29-33-33-33**) sts.

Work 2½" [6 cm] in Twisted Ribbing Pat as given for Back, ending on a 2nd row and inc 2 sts evenly across last row. **31** (**31-31-35-35-35**) sts.

Change to larger needles and proceed in pat as follows:

1st row: (RS). P**2** (**2-2-0-0-0**). (K2. P2) **1** (**1-1-2-2-2**) time(s). P2. K1tbl. Work 1st row Cable Panel A. K1tbl. P2. (P2. K2) **1** (**1-1-2-2-2**) time(s). P**2** (**2-2-0-0-0**).

2nd row: K**2** (**2-2-0-0-0**). (P2. K2) **1** (**1-1-2-2-2**) time(s). K2. P1tbl. Work 2nd row Cable Panel A. P1tbl. K2. (K2. P2) **1** (**1-1-2-2-2**) time(s). K**2** (**2-2-0-0-0**).

3rd row: K**2** (**2-2-0-0-0**). (P2. K2) **1** (**1-1-2-2-2**) time(s). P2. K1tbl. Work 3rd row Cable Panel A. K1tbl. P2. (K2. P2) **1** (**1-1-2-2-2**) time(s). K**2** (**2-2-0-0-0**).

4th row: P**2** (**2-2-0-0-0**). (K2. P2) **1** (**1-1-2-2-2**) time(s). K2. P1tbl. Work 4th row Cable Panel A. P1tbl. K2. (P2. K2) **1** (**1-1-2-2-2**) time(s). P**2** (**2-2-0-0-0**).

Last 4 rows form Box St Pat at sides. Cable Panel A is now in position.

Cont in pat, inc 1 st each end of next row and every following 4th row until there are **43** (**43-47-49-51-53**) sts, taking inc sts into Box St Pat.

Cont even in pat until work from beg measures **18** (**18-17½-17½-17-16½**)" [**45.5** (**45.5-44.5-44.5-43-42**) cm], ending with a WS row.

Shape raglans: Keeping cont of pat, cast off **2** (**2-2-3-3-3**) sts beg next 2 rows. **39** (**39-43-43-45-47**) sts rem.

Sizes L and XL only: 1st row: (RS). K2. ssk. Pat to last 4 sts. K2tog. K2.

2nd row: P2. P2tog. Pat to last 4 sts. P2togtbl. P2.

3rd row: As 1st row.

4th row: P3. Pat to last 3 sts. P3. 37 sts rem.

All sizes: 1st row: (RS). K2. ssk. Pat to last 4 sts. K2tog. K2.

2nd row: P3. Pat to last 3 sts. P3.

Rep last 2 rows 15 (15-14-14-17-18) times more.

Cast off rem 7 (7-7-7-9-9) sts.

FINISHING

Sew raglan seams.

Button and Buttonhole Band: With smaller needles, cast on 7 sts.

1st row: (RS). K1. (K1tbl. P1) twice. K1tbl. K1.

2nd row: K1. (P1tb1. K1) twice. P1tbl. K1.

Rep last 2 rows until band (when slightly stretched) measures length to fit up left front edge to beg of front shaping, sewing in place as you knit.

Mark positions for 5 buttons on this band having top button ½" [1 cm] below first front dec, bottom button ½" [1 cm] above cast on edge and rem 3 buttons spaced evenly between.

Cont in ribbing to measure up left front neck edge, across top of left sleeve, back neck edge and top of right sleeve. Cont down right front neck edge to corresponding buttonhole position.

Buttonhole row: (RS). Rib across 3 sts. yo. K2tog. Rib across 2 sts.

Cont in ribbing to measure down right front edge to cast on edge. Cast off in ribbing.

Sew side and sleeve seams. Sew on buttons.

HAT

With smaller needles, cast on 53 sts.

1st row: (RS). *P1. K1tbl. Rep from * to last st. P1.

2nd row: *K1. P1tbl. Rep from * to last st. K1.

Rep last 2 rows Twisted Ribbing Pat for 1½" [4 cm], ending on a 2nd row.

Next row: (fold line). Knit.

Beg on a 1st row (RS is now reversed for cuff turnback), work in Twisted Ribbing Pat for 1½" [4 cm], from fold line, ending on a 2nd row and inc 8 sts evenly across last row. 61 sts.

Change to larger needles and proceed in pat as follows: (See chart III on page 36).

1st row: (RS). (P1. K1) twice. *P1. Work 1st row Cable Panel B. P1. (K1. P1) 3 times. K1. Rep from * once more. P1. Work 1st row Cable Panel B. P1. (K1. P1) twice.

2nd row: (K1. P1) twice. *K1. Work 2nd row Cable Panel B. K1. (P1. K1) 3 times. P1. Rep from * once more. K1. Work 2nd row Cable Panel B. K1. (P1. K1) twice.

Shape top: 1st row: (RS). Pat across 4 sts. *P2tog. Cr4F. K1. Cr4B. P2tog. Pat across 7 sts. Rep from * once more. P2tog. Cr4F. K1. Cr4B. P2tog. Pat across last 4 sts. 55 sts.

2nd and 4th rows: Knit all knit sts and purl all purl sts as they appear.

3rd row: Pat across 4 sts. *P1. (K2tog) twice. K1. (K2tog) twice. P1. Pat across 7 sts. Rep from * once more. P1. (K2tog) twice. K1. (K2tog) twice. P1. Pat across last 4 sts. 43 sts.

5th row: (K2tog) twice. *P1. K1. Sl1. K2tog. psso. K1. P1. (K2tog) 3 times. K1. Rep from * once more. P1. K1. Sl1. K2tog. psso. K1. P1. (K2tog) twice. 27 sts.

6th row: (P2tog) 13 times. P1. 14 sts. Break yarn leaving a long end. Draw end tightly through rem sts and fasten securely. Sew center back seam.

3rd row: (K1. P1) twice. *P1. Work 1st row Cable Panel B. P1. (P1. K1) 3 times. P1. Rep from * once more. P1. Work 1st row Cable Panel B. P1. (P1. K1) twice.

4th row: (P1. K1) twice. *P1. Work 4th row Cable Panel B. P1. (K1. P1) 3 times. K1. Rep from * once more. P1. Work 4th row Cable Panel B. P1. (K1. P1) twice.

These 4 rows form Irish Moss St Pat. Cable Panel B is now in position.

Cont in pat until work from beg measures approx 8½" [21.5 cm] ending on a 4th row of Cable Panel B pat.

Pom-pom: Pom-pom: Wind 2 strands of yarn around 4 fingers approx 60 times. Remove from fingers and tie tightly in center. Cut through each side of loops. Trim to a smooth round shape (approx 4" [10 cm] diameter). Sew to top of Hat. **BERNAT**

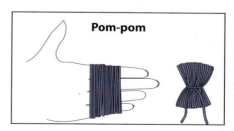

Pom-pom

Chart II

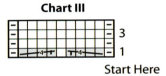

17
15
13
11
9
7
5
3
1

Start Here

Chart III

3
1

Start Here

Key

☐ = Knit on RS rows. Purl on WS rows.
⊟ = Purl on RS rows. Knit on WS rows.
= Cr4B
= Cr4F
= K1tbl on RS rows. P1tbl on WS rows.
= T2B
= T2F
= T3F

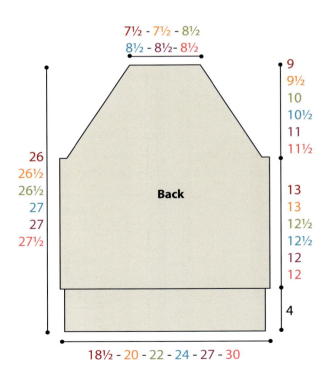

7½ - 7½ - 8½
8½ - 8½ - 8½

9
9½
10
10½
11
11½

26
26½
26½
27
27
27½

Back

13
13
12½
12½
12
12

4

18½ - 20 - 22 - 24 - 27 - 30

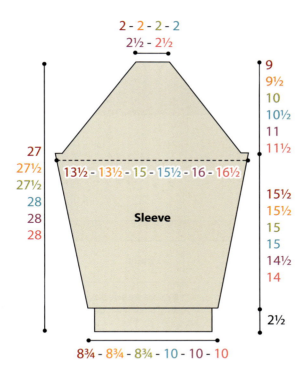

2 - 2 - 2 - 2
2½ - 2½

9
9½
10
10½
11
11½

27
27½
27½
28
28
28

13½ - 13½ - 15 - 15½ - 16 - 16½

Sleeve

15½
15½
15
15
14½
14

2½

8¾ - 8¾ - 8¾ - 10 - 10 - 10

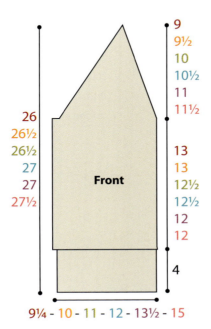

9
9½
10
10½
11
11½

26
26½
26½
27
27
27½

Front

13
13
12½
12½
12
12

4

9¼ - 10 - 11 - 12 - 13½ - 15

5. Handsome Scarf

SUPER BULKY

EASY

MEASUREMENTS
Approx 6" x 75" [18 x 190.5 cm].

GAUGE
9 sts and 12 rows = 4" [10 cm] in stocking st.

MATERIALS

Bernat® Softee® Chunky™ (100 g/3.5 oz; 99 m/108 yds)		
⬛	28013 (Dark Taupe)	**3 balls**
Size 10 mm (U.S. 15) knitting needles **or size needed to obtain gauge.**		

ABBREVIATIONS
See page 65 for Helpful Hints.
Approx = Approximately.
Beg = Beginning.
K = Knit.
K2tog = Knit next 2 stitches together.
P2tog = Purl next 2 stitches together.
Rep = Repeat.
RS = Right side.
St(s) = Stitch(es).
Tog = Together.

INSTRUCTIONS
Cast on 17 sts.

1st row: (RS). Knit.

2nd row: K1. *P2tog without slipping sts off needle, then K2tog same 2 sts. Slip sts off needle. Rep from * to end of row.

3rd row: Knit.

4th row: *P2tog without slipping sts off needle, then K2tog same 2 sts. Slip sts off needle. Rep from * to last st. K1.

Rep last 4 rows until work from beg measures 75" [190.5 cm], ending with a 1st or 3rd row. Cast off.

Fringe
Cut lengths of yarn 16" [40.5 cm] long. Taking 2 strands tog, fold in half and knot into fringe evenly across end of Scarf. Trim fringe evenly. **BERNAT**

6. Chill-Chaser Set

SUPER BULKY | **INTERMEDIATE**

MEASUREMENTS

Mittens: One size to fit average lady.

Cowl: Approx 15" [38 cm] wide x 59" [150 cm] around.

GAUGES

Mittens: 13 sts and 16 rows = 4" [10 cm] with 6.5 mm (U.S. 10½) needles in stocking st.

Cowl: 11 sts and 14 rows = 4" [10 cm] with 8 mm (U.S. 11) needles in stocking st.

MATERIALS

Bernat® Softee® Chunky™ (100 g/3.5 oz; 99 m/108 yds)		
	Mittens: 28630 (Pumpkin)	**1 ball**
Sizes 5.5 mm (U.S. 9) and 6.5 mm (U.S. 10½) knitting needles **or size needed to obtain gauge.**		
	Cowl: 28630 (Pumpkin)	**5 balls**
Size 8 mm (U.S. 11) knitting needles **or size needed to obtain gauge.** Cable needle.		

INSTRUCTIONS

MITTENS

RIGHT MITTEN

**With smaller (5.5 mm) needles, cast on 23 sts.

1st row: (RS). *K1. P1. Rep from * to last st. K1.

2nd row: *P1. K1. Rep from * to last st. P1. Rep last 2 rows (K1. P1) ribbing for 2½" [6 cm], inc 2 sts evenly across last WS row. 25 sts.**

Change to larger (6.5 mm) needles.

1st row: (RS). K2. P10. K13.

2nd row: P13. K1. *P3tog. (K1. P1. K1) all in next st. Rep from * once more. K1. P2.

3rd row: As 1st row.

4th row: P13. K1. *(K1. P1. K1) all in next st. P3tog. Rep from * once more. K1. P2.

Last 4 rows form pat.

Work a further 4 rows in pat.

Shape thumb gusset: 1st row: (RS). Pat across 13 sts. Inc 1 st in each of next 2 sts. Knit to end of row.

2nd and following alt rows: Work even in pat.

3rd row: Pat across 13 sts. Inc 1 st in next st. K2. Inc 1 st in next st. Knit to end of row.

5th row: Pat across 13 sts. Inc 1 st in next st. K4. Inc 1 st in next st. Knit to end of row. 31 sts.

6th row: As 2nd row.

Shape thumb: Next row: (RS). Pat across 21 sts. **Turn.** Leave rem sts on a spare needle.

***Next row:** Cast on 1 st. P9 (including cast on st). **Turn.** Leave rem sts on a spare needle.

Next row: Cast on 1 st. K10 (including cast on st).

Work a further 5 rows in stocking st on these 10 sts.

Next row: (RS). (K2tog) 5 times. 5 sts.

Next row: (P2tog) twice. P1. 3 sts. Break yarn, leaving a long end. Draw end tightly through rem sts. Sew thumb seam.

Next row: (RS). Rejoin yarn. Pick up and knit 2 sts over cast on sts at base of thumb. Pat to end of row across sts from spare needle. 25 sts.***

Cont in pat until work from beg measures approx 9½" [24 cm], ending with the following pat row:
Last row: (WS). P13. K1. *P3tog. (K1. P1. K1) all in next st. Rep from * once more. K1. P2.

Shape top: 1st row: (RS). K2. P10. ssk. K2tog. K6. ssk. K1. 22 sts.
2nd row: P10. K2. (P3tog. K1) twice. P2. 18 sts.
3rd row: K2tog. (P2tog) 3 times. (K2tog) 5 times. 9 sts. Break yarn leaving a long end. Draw end tightly through rem sts. Sew side seam.

LEFT MITTEN

Work from ** to ** as given for Right Mitten.

Change to larger (6.5 mm) needles.
1st row: (RS). K13. P10. K2.
2nd row: P2. K1. *P3tog. (K1. P1. K1) all in next st. Rep from * once more. K1. P13.
3rd row: As 1st row.
4th row: P2. K1. *(K1. P1. K1) all in next st. P3tog. Rep from * once more. K1. P13.
Last 4 rows form pat.
Work a further 4 rows in pat.

Shape thumb gusset: 1st row: (RS). Pat across 10 sts. Inc 1 st in each of next 2 sts. Pat to end of row.

2nd and following alt rows: Work even in pat.
3rd row: Pat across 10 sts. Inc 1 st in next st. K2. Inc 1 st in next st. Knit to end of row.
5th row: Pat across 10 sts. Inc 1 st in next st. K4. Inc 1 st in next st. Knit to end of row. 31 sts.
6th row: As 2nd row.

Shape thumb: Next row: (RS). Pat across 18 sts. **Turn.** Leave rem sts on a spare needle.
Work from *** to *** as given for Right Mitten.
Cont in pat until work from beg measures approx 9½" [24 cm], ending with the following pat row:
Last row: (WS). P2. K1. *P3tog. (K1. P1. K1) all in next st. Rep from * once more. K1. P13.

Shape top: 1st row: (RS). K1. K2tog. K6. K2tog. ssk. P10. K2. 22 sts.
2nd row: P2. K2. (P3tog. K1) twice. P10. 18 sts.
3rd row: (K2tog) 5 times. (P2tog) 3 times. K2tog. 9 sts. Break yarn, leaving a long end. Draw end tightly through rem sts. Sew side seam.

COWL

Cable Panel (worked over 21 sts).
(See Chart IV on page 44).
1st row: (RS). K6. P2. K2tog. yo. P1. yo. ssk. P2. K6.
2nd row: P6. K2. P2. K1. P2. K2. P6.
3rd row: C6F. P2. yo. ssk. P1. K2tog. yo. P2. C6B.

4th row: As 2nd row.

5th and 6th rows: As 1st and 2nd rows.

7th row: K6. P2. yo. ssk. P1. K2tog. yo. P2. K6.

8th row: As 2nd row.

9th row: C6F. P2. K2tog. yo. P1. yo. ssk. P2. C6B.

10th row: As 2nd row.

11th row: As 7th row.

12th row: (P2. K2) twice. P2. K1. (P2. K2) twice. P2.

13th row: yo. ssk. P2. K6. P1. K6. P2. K2tog. yo.

14th row: P2. K2. P6. K1. P6. K2. P2.

15th row: K2tog. yo. P2. C6B. P1. C6F. P2. yo. ssk.

16th row: As 14th row.

17th and 18th rows: As 13th and 14th rows.

19th row: K2tog. yo. P2. K6. P1. K6. P2. yo. ssk.

20th row: As 14th row.

21st row: yo. ssk. P2. C6B. P1. C6F. P2. K2tog. yo.

22nd row: As 14th row.

23rd row: As 19th row.

24th row: As 12th row.

These 24 rows form Cable Panel pat.

With 8 mm needles, cast on 45 sts.

1st row: (RS). K2. P10. Work 1st row of Cable Panel across next 21 sts. P10. K2.

2nd row: K2. *P3tog. (K1. P1. K1) all in next st. Rep from * once more. K2. Work 2nd row of Cable Panel across next 21 sts. K2. **(K1. P1. K1) all in next st. P3tog. Rep from ** once more. K2.

3rd row: K2. P10. Work 3rd row of Cable Panel across next 21 sts. P10. K2.

4th row: K2. *(K1. P1. K1) all in next st. P3tog. Rep from * once more. K2. Work 4th row of Cable Panel across next 21 sts. K2. **P3tog. (K1. P1. K1) all in next st. Rep from ** once more. K2.

These 4 rows form Trinity St pat. Cable Panel is now in position.

Cont in pat, keeping cont of Cable Panel, until work from beg measures approx 59" [150 cm] ending on a 10th row of Cable Panel pat. Cast off in pat. Sew cast on and cast off edges tog.

Sew center back seam. **BERNAT**

Chart IV

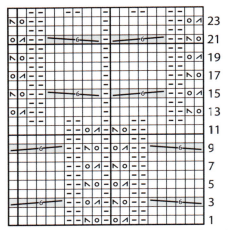

Start Here

Key

☐ = Knit on RS rows.
  Purl on WS rows.

⊟ = Purl on RS rows.
  Knit on WS rows.

⬜⬜⬜⬜⬜⬜ = C6B

⬜⬜⬜⬜⬜⬜ = C6F

◙ = yo

◩ = ssk

◪ = K2tog

7. Into the Woods Coat

SUPER BULKY   INTERMEDIATE

SIZES

To fit bust measurement
Extra-Small/Small   28-34" [71-86.5 cm]
Medium   36-38" [91.5-96.5 cm]
Large   40-42" [101.5-106.5 cm]
Extra-Large   44-46" [112-117 cm]
2/3 Extra-Large   48-54" [122-137 cm]
4/5 Extra-Large   56-62" [142-157.5 cm]

Finished bust	
Extra-Small/Small: 43" [109 cm]	
Medium:	45" [114.5 cm]
Large:	50" [127 cm]
Extra-Large:	52" [132 cm]
2/3 Extra-Large:	58" [147.5 cm]
4/5 Extra-Large:	65" [165 cm]

GAUGE

11 sts and 14 rows = 4" [10 cm] with larger needles in stocking st.

MATERIALS

Bernat® Softee® Chunky™ (100 g/3.5 oz; 99 m/108 yds)								
Cardigan Sizes	XS/S	M	L	XL	2/3XL	4/5XL	
28247 (Eucalyptus)	14	15	16	17	18	19	**balls**

Sizes 6.5 mm (U.S. 10½) and 8 mm (U.S. 11) knitting needles **or size needed to obtain gauge.** Cable needle. 2 st holders. 5 buttons.

ABBREVIATIONS

See page 65 for Helpful Hints.
Alt = Alternate(ing).
Approx = Approximately.
Beg = Beginning.
C4B = Slip next 2 stitches onto cable needle and leave at back of work. K2, then K2 from cable needle.
C4F = Slip next 2 stitches onto cable needle and leave at front of work. K2, then K2 from cable needle.
Cont = Continue(ity).
Dec = Decrease(ing).
Inc(s) = Increase 1 stitch by knitting into front and back of next stitch.

K = Knit.
K2tog = Knit next 2 stitches together.
M1P = Make 1 stitch by picking up horizontal loop lying before next stitch and purling into back of loop.
P = Purl.
Pat = Pattern.
Rem = Remaining.
Rep = Repeat.
RS = Right side.
St(s) = Stitch(es).
T4B = Slip next 2 stitches onto cable needle and leave at back of work. K2, then P2 from cable needle.

T4F = Slip next 2 stitches onto cable needle and leave at front of work. P2, then K2 from cable needle.
T6B = Slip next 4 stitches onto cable needle and leave at back of work. K2, then P2. K2 from cable needle.
T6F = Slip next 2 stitches onto cable needle and leave at front of work. K2. P2, then K2 from cable needle.
WS = Wrong side.
Yo = Yarn over.

INSTRUCTIONS

The instructions are written for smallest size. If changes are necessary for larger sizes the instructions will be written thus ( ). Numbers for each size are shown in the same color throughout the pattern. When only one number is given in black, it applies to all sizes.

CABLE PANEL A (worked over 10 sts).
(See Chart V on page 51).
1st row: (RS). (K2. P2) twice. K2.

2nd and alt rows: Knit all knit sts and purl all purl sts as they appear.
3rd row: As 1st row.
5th row: K2. P2. K2. C4B.
7th row: K2. P2. T4B. K2.
9th row: K2. T4B. P2. K2.
11th row: T4B. P2. C4B.
13th row: K2. P2. T4B. K2.
15th row: K2. C4B. P2. K2.
17th row: T4B. K2. P2. K2.
19th and 20th rows: As 1st and 2nd rows.
These 20 rows form Cable Panel A.

CABLE PANEL B (worked over 10 sts).

(See Chart VI on page 51).

1st row: (RS). (K2. P2) twice. K2.

2nd and alt rows: Knit all knit sts and purl all purl sts as they appear.

3rd row: As 1st row.

5th row: C4F. K2. P2. K2.

7th row: K2. T4F. P2. K2.

9th row: K2. P2. T4F. K2.

11th row: C4F. P2. T4F.

13th row: K2. T4F. P2. K2.

15th row: K2. P2. C4F. K2.

17th row: K2. P2. K2. T4F.

19th and 20th rows: As 1st and 2nd rows. These 20 rows form Cable Panel B.

CABLE PANEL C (worked over 12 sts).

(See Chart VII on page 51).

1st row: (RS). (K2. P2) 3 times.

2nd and alt rows: (K2. P2) 3 times.

3rd row: T6B. P2. K2. P2.

5th row: As 1st row.

7th row: K2. P2. T6F. P2.

8th row: As 2nd row.

These 8 rows form Cable Panel C.

BACK

With larger needles, cast on **82** (**86**-**94**-**98**-**108**-**118**) sts.

1st row: (RS). *K2. P2. Rep from * to last 2 sts. K2.

2nd row: *P2. K2. Rep from * to last 2 sts. P2. Rep last 2 rows (K2. P2) ribbing for 3½" [9 cm], ending on a 2nd row and inc **4** (**4**-**4**-**6**-**8**-**10**) sts evenly across last row. **86** (**90**-**98**-**104**-**116**-**128**) sts.

Proceed in pat as follows:

1st row: (RS). P**2** (**4**-**2**-**5**-**5**-**5**). *Work 1st row Cable Panel C. Rep from * to last **0** (**2**-**0**-**3**-**3**-**3**) sts. P**0** (**2**-**0**-**3**-**3**-**3**).

2nd row: K**0** (**2**-**0**-**3**-**3**-**3**). *Work 2nd row Cable Panel C. Rep from * to last **2** (**4**-**2**-**5**-**5**-**5**) sts. K**2** (**4**-**2**-**5**-**5**-**5**).

Cable Panel C is now in position.

Cont even in pat, until work from beg measures **23** (**23**-**22½**-**22½**-**22**-**22**)" [**58.5** (**58.5**-**57**-**57**-**56**- **56**) cm], ending with a WS row.

Shape armholes: Keeping cont of pat, cast off **13** (**14**-**13**-**16**-**18**-**18**) sts beg next 2 rows. **60** (**62**-**72**-**72**-**80**-**92**) sts rem.

Cont even in pat until armhole measures **9** (**9½**-**10**-**10**-**10½**-**10½**)" [**23** (**24**-**25.5**-**25.5**-**26.5**-**26.5**) cm], ending with a WS row.

Shape shoulders: Keeping cont of pat, cast off **8** (**8**-**11**-**11**-**12**-**15**) sts beg next 2 rows, then cast off **8** (**9**-**11**-**11**-**12**-**15**) sts beg following 2 rows. Leave rem **28** (**28**-**28**-**28**-**32**-**32**) sts on a st holder.

LEFT FRONT

With larger needles, cast on **44** (**44**-**52**-**56**-**56**-**64**) sts.

1st row: (RS). (K2. P2) **8** (**8**-**10**-**11**-**11**-**13**) times. Work 1st row Cable Panel A. P2.

2nd row: K2. Work 2nd row Cable Panel A. (K2. P2) **8** (**8**-**10**-**11**-**11**-**13**) times.

Last 2 rows form (K2. P2) ribbing and Cable Panel A.

Cable Panel A is now in position.

Cont even in pat for 3½" [9 cm], ending with a RS row.

Next row: (WS). K2. Work appropriate row Cable Panel A. K2. P3 (5-6-5-5-7). [M1P. P5 (3-3-4-4-3) 5 (7-9-8-8-12) times. M1P. P2 (4-5-5-5-7). 50 (52-62-65-65-77) sts.

Proceed in pat as follows:

1st row: (RS). P2 (4-2-5-5-5). (Work 1st row Cable Panel C) 3 (3-4-4-4-5) times. Work appropriate row Cable Panel A. P2.

2nd row: K2. Work appropriate row Cable Panel A. (Work 2nd row Cable Panel C) 3 (3-4-4-4-5) times. K2 (4-2-5-5-5).
Cable Panels A and C are now in position.

Cont even in pat until work from beg measures 23 (23-22½-22½-22-22)" [58.5 (58.5-57-57-56-56) cm], ending with a WS row.

Shape armhole: Keeping cont of pat, cast off 13 (14-13-16-18-18) sts beg next row. 37 (38-49-49-47-59) sts rem.
Cont even in pat until armhole measures 6 (6½-7-7-7½-7½)" [15 (16.5-18-18-19-19) cm], ending with a RS row.

Shape neck: Next row: (WS). Pat across next 14 (14-18-18-18-18) sts. Slip last 14 (14-14-14-18-18) sts onto a st holder. Pat to end of row.
Keeping cont of pat, dec 1 st at neck edge on next 7 (7-9-9-5-11) rows. 16 (17-22-22-24-30) sts rem.

Cont even in pat until armhole measures 9 (9½-10-10-10½-10½)" [23 (24-25.5-25.5-26.5-26.5) cm], ending with a WS row.

Shape shoulder: Keeping cont of pat, cast off 8 (8-11-11-12-15) sts beg next row. Work 1 row even in pat.
Cast off rem 8 (9-11-11-12-15) sts.

RIGHT FRONT
With larger needles, cast on 44 (44-52-56-56-64) sts.

1st row: (RS). P2. Work 1st row Cable Panel B. (P2. K2) 8 (8-10-11-11-13) times.

2nd row: (P2. K2) 8 (8-10-11-11-13) times. Work 2nd row Cable Panel B. K2.
Last 2 rows form (K2. P2) ribbing and Cable Panel B.

Cont even in pat for 3½" [9 cm], ending with a RS row.

Next row: (WS). P2 (4-5-5-5-7). [M1P. P5 (3-3-4-4-3)] 5 (7-9-8-8-12) times. M1P. P3 (5-6-5-5-7). K2. Work appropriate row Cable Panel B. K2. 50 (52-62-65-65-77) sts.

Proceed in pat as follows:

1st row: (RS). P2. Work appropriate row Cable Panel B. P2. (Work 1st row Cable Panel C) 3 (3-4-4-4-5) times. P0 (2-0-3-3-3).

2nd row: K0 (2-0-3-3-3). (Work 2nd row Cable Panel C) 3 (3-4-4-4-5) times. K2. Work appropriate row Cable Panel B. K2.
Cable Panel C is now in position.

Cont even in pat until work from beg measures 23 (23-22½-22½-22-22)" [58.5 (58.5-57-57-56- 5 6) cm], ending with a RS row.

Shape armhole: Keeping cont of pat, cast off 13 (14-13-16-18-18) sts beg next row. 37 (38-49-49-47-59) sts rem.
Cont even in pat until armhole measures 6 (6½-7-7-7½-8)" [15 (16.5-18-18-19-20.5) cm], ending with a RS row.

Shape neck: Next row: (RS). Pat across next 14 (14-18-18-18-18) sts. Slip last 14 (14-18-18-18-18) sts onto a st holder. Pat to end of row.
Keeping cont of pat, dec 1 st at neck edge on next 7 (7-9-9-5-11) rows. 16 (17-22-22-24-30) sts rem.

Cont even in pat until armhole measures 9 (9½-10-10-10½-10½)" [23 (24.5-25.5-25.5-26.5-26.5) cm], ending with a RS row.

Shape shoulder: Keeping cont of pat, cast off 8 (8-11-11-12-15) sts beg next row. Work 1 row even in pat.
Cast off rem 8 (9-11-11-12-15) sts.

SLEEVES

With smaller needles, cast on 42 (42-42-42-54-54) sts. Work 3" [7.5 cm] in (K2. P2) ribbing as given for Back, ending on a 2nd row and inc 8 sts evenly across. 50 (50-50-50-62-62) sts.

Change to larger needles and proceed in pat as follows:
1st row: (RS). P2. *Work 1st row Cable Panel C. Rep from * to end of row.
2nd row: *Work 2nd row Cable Panel C. Rep from * to last 2 sts. K2.
Cable Panel C is now in position.

Cont even in pat for 4 more rows.
Inc 1 st each end of next and every following 4th row until there are 74 (76-78-78-82-82) sts, taking inc sts into Cable Panel C pat (noting that inc sts will be taken into reverse stocking st after 74 sts in pat.

Cont even in pat until work from beg measures 17½ (17½-17-17-16½-16½)" [44.5 (44.5-43-43-42-42) cm], ending with a WS row. Place markers at each end of last row. Work 10 (12-10-12-14-14) rows even in pat. Cast off in pat.

FINISHING

Pin all pieces to measurements. Cover with a damp cloth, leaving cloth to dry.
Sew shoulder seams.

Buttonhole Band: With RS facing and smaller needles, pick up and knit 74 (78-78-82-82-82) sts up Right Front edge between cast on edge and neck edge.
Knit 1 row.
Next row: K14. [K2tog. yo. K12 (13-13-14-14-14)] 4 times. K2tog. yo. K2. 5 buttonholes made.
Cast off knitwise (WS).

Button Band: With RS facing and smaller needles, pick up and knit **74** (**78**-**78**-**82**-**82**-**82**) sts down Left Front edge between neck edge and cast on edge.

Knit 2 rows.

Cast off knitwise (WS).

COLLAR

With RS facing and smaller needles, work across **14** (**14**-**18**-**18**-**18**-**18**) sts from Right Front st holder as follows: P2. (K2. K2tog) **3** (**3**-**4**-**4**-**4**-**4**) times. Pick up and knit 12 sts up Right Front neck edge. Knit across **28** (**28**-**28**-**28**-**32**-**32**) sts from Back st holder, dec **4** (**4**-**2**-**2**-**2**-**2**) sts evenly across . Pick up and knit 12 sts down Left Front neck edge. Work across **14** (**14**-**18**-**18**-**18**-**18**) sts from Right Front st holder as follows: (K2tog. K2) **3** (**3**-**4**-**4**-**4**-**4**) times. P2. **70** (**70**-**78**-**78**-**82**-**82**) sts.

1st row: (WS). *K2. P2. Rep from * to last 2 sts. K2.

2nd row: *P2. K2. Rep from * to last 2 sts. P2.

Rep last 2 rows until Collar measures 5" [12.5 cm], ending on a 1st row. Cast off loosely in ribbing.

Sew in Sleeves, placing rows above markers along cast off sts of Back and Fronts to form square armholes.

Sew side and sleeve seams. Sew on buttons to correspond to buttonholes. **BERNAT**

Chart V

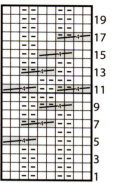

Start Here

Chart VI

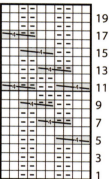

Start Here

Chart VII

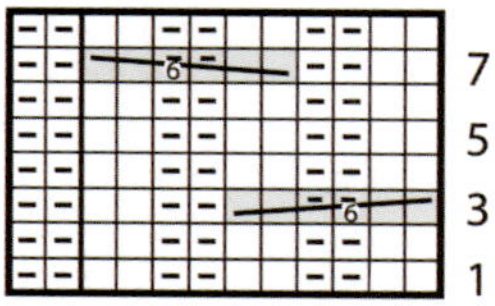

Start Here

Key

□	= Knit on RS rows. Purl on WS rows.
⊟	= Purl on RS rows. Knit on WS rows.
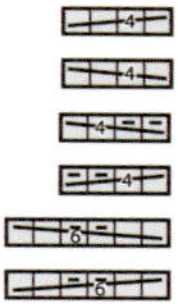	= C4B
	= C4F
	= T4F
	= T4B
	= T6F
	= T6B

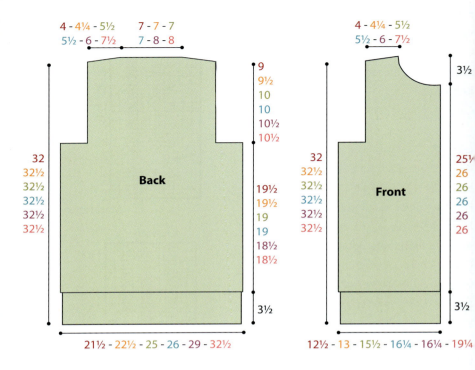

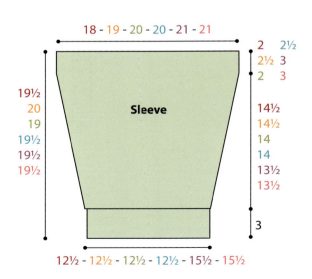

8. Retro Spirit Jacket

 CIRCULAR NEEDLE   SUPER BULKY   INTERMEDIATE

SIZES

To fit chest measurement
Extra-Small/Small 28-34" [71-86.5 cm]
Medium 36-38" [91.5-96.5 cm]
Large 40-42" [101.5-106.5 cm]
Extra-Large 44-46" [112-117 cm]
2/3 Extra-Large 48-54" [122-137 cm]
4/5 Extra-Large 56-62" [142-157.5 cm]

Finished chest		
Extra-Small/Small:	36"	[91.5 cm]
Medium:	40"	[101.5 cm]
Large:	44"	[112 cm]
Extra-Large:	48"	[122 cm]
2/3 Extra-Large:	55"	[139.5 cm]
4/5 Extra-Large:	63"	[160 cm]

GAUGE

11 sts and 14 rows = 4" [10 cm] with larger needles in stocking st.

Note: For Hat pattern see page 24 (#3. Unisex Classic Set).

MATERIALS

Bernat® Softee® Chunky (100 g/3.5 oz; 99 m/108 yds)								
Cardigan Sizes		**XS/S**	**M**	**L**	**XL**	**2/3XL**	**4/5XL**	
	Main Color (MC) (28013 Dark Taupe)	6	6	7	7	8	8	**balls**
	Contrast A (28008 Natural)	2	2	2	2	3	3	**balls**
	Contrast B (28044 True Grey)	2	2	2	2	2	2	**balls**
	Contrast C (28011 Soft Taupe)	1	1	1	1	2	2	**ball(s)**

Sizes 6.5 mm (U.S. 10½) and 8 mm (U.S. 11) knitting needles. Size 6.5 mm (U.S. 10½) circular knitting needle 24" [60 cm] long **or size needed to obtain gauge.** 3 stitch holders. Separating zipper approx **20** (**20**-**22**-**22**-**22**-**23½**)" [**50** (**50**-**55**-**55**-**55**-**60**) cm] long.

ABBREVIATIONS

See page 65 for Helpful Hints.

Beg = Beginning.

Cont = Continue(ity).

Dec = Decrease(ing).

Inc = Increase 1 stitch by knitting into front and back of next stitch.

K = Knit.

K2tog = Knit next 2 stitches together.

M1 = Make 1 stitch by picking up horizontal loop lying before next stitch and knitting into back of loop.

P = Purl.

P2tog = Purl next 2 stitches together.

P2togtbl = Purl next 2 stitches together through back loops.

Rem = Remaining.

Rep = Repeat.

RS = Right side.

Ssk = Slip next 2 stitches knitwise one at a time. Pass them back onto left-hand needle, then knit through back loops together

St(s) = Stitch(es).

Tog = Together.

WS = Wrong side.

INSTRUCTIONS

The instructions are written for smallest size. If changes are necessary for larger sizes the instructions will be written thus ( ). Numbers for each size are shown in the same color throughout the pattern. When only one number is given in black, it applies to all sizes.

Notes: Body is worked in one piece to armholes.

When working from Charts VIII, XII, XIII and XIV, carry color not in use loosely across WS of work but never more than over 3 sts. When it must pass over more than 3 sts, weave it under and over color in use.

Note: When working from Charts IX, X and XI, wind small balls of the colors to be used, one for each separate area of color in the design. When changing colors, wind the 2 colors around each other where they meet, on WS, to avoid a hole.

BODY
With MC and smaller circular needle, cast on **98 (**110**-**118**-**130**-**150**-**174**) sts. **Do not join.** Working back and forth across needle in rows, proceed as follows:
1st row: (RS). *K2. P2. Rep from * to last 2 sts. K2.
2nd row: *P2. K2. Rep from * to last 2 sts. P2.
Rep last 2 rows (K2. P2) ribbing for 2½" [6 cm], ending on a 2nd row and inc **2** (**0**-**2**-**2**-**2**-**0**) sts evenly across last row. **100** (**110**-**120**-**132**-**150**-**174**) sts.

Change to larger circular needle and work 4 rows stocking st, inc 8 sts evenly across last WS row. **108** (**118**-**128**-**140**-**158**-**182**) sts.

Work Chart VIII (see chart on page 61) in stocking st to end of chart, reading **knit** rows from **right** to left and **purl** rows from **left** to right, noting 6-st rep will be worked **18** (**19**-**21**-**23**-**26**-**30**) times.
Next row: (WS). With MC, purl dec 7 sts evenly across. **101** (**111**-**121**-**133**-**151**-**175**) sts.

Placing Charts IX, X and XI: (See page 62)
1st row: (RS). With A, K**2** (**3**-**3**-**3**-**4**-**4**). Knit 1st row of Chart IX across 20 sts, reading row from **right** to left. K**6** (**10**-**15**-**21**-**29**-**41**). Knit 1st row of Chart X across 45 sts, reading row from **right** to left. K**6** (**10**-**15**-**21**-**29**-**41**). Knit 1st row of Chart XI across 20 sts, reading row from **right** to left. With A, K**2** (**3**-**3**-**3**-**4**-**4**).
2nd row: With A, P**2** (**3**-**3**-**3**-**4**-**4**). Purl 2nd row of Chart XI across 20 sts, reading row from **left** to right. P**6** (**10**-**15**-**21**-**29**-**41**). Purl 2nd row of Chart X across 45 sts, reading row from **left** to right. P**6** (**10**-**15**-**21**-**29**-**41**). Purl 2nd row of Chart IX across 20 sts, reading row from **left** to right. With A, P**2** (**3**-**3**-**3**-**4**-**4**).
Charts IX, X and XI are now in position.

Work charts to end of Charts IX, X and XI.
Next row: (WS). With MC, purl, inc 7 sts evenly across. **108** (**118**-**128**-**140**-**158**-**182**) sts.

Work Chart XII (see page 62) in stocking st until 8th row of chart has been completed, reading **knit** rows from **right** to left and **purl** rows from **left** to right, noting 6-st rep will be worked **18** (**19**-**21**-**23**-**26**-**30**) times.

Divide for armholes: Next row: (RS). Keeping cont of chart, pat **25** (**28**-**29**-**31**-**36**-**42**) sts. Cast off next **4** (**4**-**6**-**8**-**8**-**8**) sts. Pat **50** (**54**-**58**-**62**-**70**-**82**) sts (including st on needle after cast off). Cast off next **4** (**4**-**6**-**8**-**8**-**8**) sts. Pat **25** (**28**-**29**-**31**-**36**-**42**) sts (including st on needle after cast off).

Left Front: Cont on last **25** (**28**-29-31-**36**-42) sts. Cont working Chart XII to end of chart as follows:

Sizes XS/S, M, L, XL and 2/3XL only: Shape raglan: 1st row: (WS). Purl.
2nd row: K1. ssk. Pat to end of row.
Rep last 2 rows 3 times more, then 1st row once. **21** (**24**-25-27-**32**) sts.

With MC only, rep last 2 rows **2** (**3**-5-6-**6**) times more. **19** (**21**-20-21-**26**) sts.

Sizes XS/S, M, L and XL only:
Shape neck: 1st row: (RS). K1. ssk. Knit to end of row.
2nd row: P**2** (**3**-3-**3**). Slip these **2** (**3**-3-**3**) sts onto a st holder. Purl to end of row. **16** (**17**-16-**17**) sts rem.
3rd row: K1. ssk. Knit to last 3 sts. K2tog. K1.
4th row: P1. P2tog. Purl to end of row.
Rep last 2 rows **1** (**2**-1-**2**) time(s) more. **10** (**8**-10-**8**) sts rem.

Next row: (RS). K1. ssk. Knit to last 3 sts. K2tog. K1.
Next row: Purl.
Rep last 2 rows **1** (**0**-1-**0**) time more. 6 sts rem.

Next row: (RS). K1. ssk. K2tog. K1.
Next row: Purl.
Next row: ssk. K2tog.
Next row: Purl.
Next row: ssk. Fasten off.

Size 4/5XL only: Shape raglan: 1st row: (WS). Purl.
2nd row: K1. ssk. Pat to end of row.
Rep last 2 rows once more, then 1st row once. 40 sts.

Proceed as follows:
1st row: (RS). K1. ssk. Pat to end of row.
2nd row: Pat to last 3 sts. P2togtbl. P1.
3rd row: As 1st row.
4th row: Work even in pat.
With MC only, rep last 4 rows 3 times more. 28 sts.

Sizes 2/3XL and 4/5XL only: Shape neck: 1st row: (RS). K1. ssk. Knit to end of row.
2nd row: P3. Slip these 3 sts onto a st holder. Purl to last 3 sts. P2togtbl. P1. (**21**-**23**) sts rem.
3rd row: K1. ssk. Knit to last 3 sts. K2tog. K1.
4th row: P1. P2tog. Purl to end of row.
5th row: As 3rd row.
6th row: P1. P2tog. Purl to last 3 sts P2togtbl. P1.
Rep last 4 rows (**0**-**1**) time more. (**14**-**9**) sts rem.

Next row: (RS). **1st row:** K1. ssk. Knit to last 3 sts. K2tog. K1. (**12**-**7**) sts rem.
2nd row: Purl.

Size 2/3XL only: 1st row: K1. ssk. Knit to last 3 sts. K2tog. K1.

2nd row: Purl to last 3 sts. P2togtbl. P1.

3rd row: As 1st row. 7 sts rem.

4th row: Purl.

Sizes 2/3XL and 4/5XL only: 1st row: K1. ssk. K1. K2tog. K1.

2nd row: P2. P2togtbl. P1.

3rd row: ssk. K2tog.

4th row: P2.

5th row: ssk. Fasten off.

Back: With WS facing, rejoin appropriate color to **50** (**54**-**58**-**62**-**70**-**82**) sts for Back. Cont working Chart XII to end of chart as follows:

Sizes XS/S, M, L, XL and 2/3XL only: Shape raglans: 1st row: (WS). Purl.

2nd row: K1. ssk. Pat to last 3 sts. K2tog. K1.

Rep last 2 rows 3 times more, then 1st row once. **42** (**46**-**50**-**54**-**62**) sts.

With MC only, proceed as follows:
Rep last 2 rows **10** (**11**-**13**-**14**-**7**) times more. **22** (**24**-**24**-**26**-**48**) sts rem.

Size 4/5XL only: Shape raglans: 1st row: (WS). Purl.

2nd row: K1. ssk. Pat to last 3 sts. K2tog. K1.

Rep last 2 rows once more, then 1st row once. **78** sts.

Sizes 2/3XL and 4/5XL only: 1st row: (RS). K1. ssk. Knit to last 3 sts. K2tog. K1.

2nd row: P1. P2togtbl. Purl to last 3 sts. P2togtbl. P1.

3rd row: As 1st row.

4th row: Purl.

Rep last 4 rows (**3**-**7**) times more. (**24**-**30**) sts rem.

All sizes: Cast off.

Right Front: With WS facing, rejoin appropriate color to rem **25** (**28**-**29**-**31**-**36**-**42**) sts. Cont in Chart V to end of chart as follows:

Sizes XS/S, M, L, XL and 2/3XL only: Shape raglan: 1st row: (WS). Purl.

2nd row: Knit to last 3 sts. K2tog. K1.

Rep last 2 rows 3 times more, then 1st row once. **21** (**24**-**25**-**27**-**32**) sts.

With MC only, rep last 2 rows **2** (**3**-**5**-**6**-**6**) times more. **19** (**21**-**20**-**21**-**26**) sts.

Sizes XS/S, M, L and XL only:
Shape neck: 1st row: (RS). K**2** (**3**-**3**-**3**). Slip these **2** (**3**-**3**-**3**) sts onto a st holder. Knit to last 3 sts. K2tog. K1. **16** (**17**-**16**-**17**) sts rem.

2nd row: Purl.

3rd row: K1. ssk. Knit to last 3 sts. K2tog. K1.

4th row: Purl to last 3 sts. P2tog. P1.

Rep last 2 rows **1** (**2**-**1**-**2**) time(s) more. **10** (**8**-**10**-**8**) sts rem.

Next row: (RS). K1. ssk. Knit to last 3 sts. K2tog. K1.

Next row: Purl.

Rep last 2 rows **1** (**0-1-0**) time more. 6 sts rem.

Next row: (RS). K1. ssk. K2tog. K1.

Next row: Purl.

Next row: ssk. K2tog.

Next row: Purl.

Next row: K2tog. Fasten off.

Size 4/5XL only: Shape raglan: 1st row: (WS). Purl.

2nd row: Knit to last 3 sts. K2tog. K1.

Rep last 2 rows once more, then 1st row once. 40 sts.

Proceed as follows:

1st row: (RS). Knit to last 3 sts. K2tog. K1.

2nd row: P1. P2tog. Purl to end of row.

3rd row: As 1st row.

4th row: Work even in pat.

With MC only, rep last 4 rows 3 times more. 28 sts.

Sizes 2/3XL and 4/5XL only: Shape neck: 1st row: (RS). K3. Slip these 3 sts onto a st holder. Knit to last 3 sts. K2tog. K1.

2nd row: P1. P2tog. Purl to end of row. (**21-23**) sts rem.

3rd row: K1. ssk. Knit to last 3 sts. K2tog. K1.

4th row: Purl to last 3 sts. P2tog. P1.

5th row: As 3rd row.

6th row: P1. P2tog. Purl to last 3 sts. P2togtbl. P1.

Rep last 4 rows (**0-1**) time more. (**14-9**) sts rem.

Next row: (RS). **1st row:** K1. ssk. Knit to last 3 sts. K2tog. K1. (**12-7**) sts rem.

2nd row: Purl.

Size 2/3XL only: 1st row: K1. ssk. Knit to last 3 sts. K2tog. K1.

2nd row: P1. P2tog. Purl to end of row.

3rd row: As 1st row. 7 sts rem.

4th row: Purl.

Sizes 2/3XL and 4/5XL only: 1st row: K1. ssk. K1. K2tog. K1.

2nd row: P1. P2togtbl. P2.

3rd row: ssk. K2tog.

4th row: P2.

5th row: ssk. Fasten off.

SLEEVES

With MC and smaller needles, cast on 30 sts.

1st row: K2. *P2. K2. Rep from * to end of row.

2nd row: P2. *K2. P2. Rep from * to end of row.

Rep last 2 rows of (K2. P2) ribbing for 2½" [6 cm], ending with a 2nd row.

Change to larger needles and work 4 rows in stocking st, inc 6 sts evenly across last row. 36 sts.

Work Chart XIII (see page 63 noting appropriate verion of chart for your size) to end of chart, reading knit rows from **right** to left and purl rows from **left** to right, noting 6-st rep will be worked 6 times, AT SAME TIME working inc at each end of **7th** (**7th**-**7th**-**1st**-**1st**-**1st**) row and every following **10th** (**10th**-**6th**-**6th**-**4th**-**4th**) row. **40** (**40**-**40**-**42**-**46**-**46**) sts.
Chart XIII is now complete.

Next row: (WS). With MC, purl, dec **6** (**6**-**6**-**4**-**4**-**4**) sts evenly across. **34** (**34**-**34**-**38**-**42**-**42**) sts.

Place Chart IX for Left Sleeve or Chart XI for Right Sleeve: (see page 63)

Sizes XS/S, M, 2/3XL and 4/5XL only:
1st row: (RS). With A, K**7** (**7**-**11**-**11**). Knit 1st row of Chart IX or XI across 20 sts. With A, K**7** (**7**-**11**-**11**).
2nd row: With A, P**7** (**7**-**11**-**11**). Purl 2nd row of Chart IX or XI across 20 sts. With A, P**7** (**7**-**11**-**11**).

Sizes L and XL only: 1st row: (RS). With A, inc 1 st in first st. K(**6**-**8**). Knit 1st row of Chart IX or XI across 20 sts. With A, K(**5**-**7**). Inc 1 st in next st. K1.
2nd row: With A, P(**8**-**10**). Purl 2nd row of Chart IX or XI across 20 sts. With A, P(**8**-**10**).

All sizes: Charts IX or XI are now in position.

Work charts to end of Charts IX or XI, inc 1 st each end of needle on every following **10th** (**10th**-**6th**-**6th**-**4th**-**4th**) row from previous inc until there are **38** (**38**-**42**-**44**-**50**-**50**) sts.
Next row: (WS). With MC, purl, inc 6 sts evenly across. **44** (**44**-**48**-**50**-**56**-**56**) sts.

Work Chart XIV in stocking st until 8th row of chart has been complete, reading **knit** rows from **right** to left and **purl** rows from **left** to right, noting 6-st rep will be worked 5 times. **44** (**46**-**50**-**52**-**56**-**58**) sts.

Shape raglans: Next row: (RS). Keeping cont of chart, cast off **2** (**2**-**3**-**4**-**4**-**4**) sts beg next 2 rows. **40** (**42**-**44**-**44**-**48**-**50**) sts.
1st row: (RS). K1. ssk. Pat to last 3 sts. K2tog. K1.
2nd row: Purl.
Rep last 2 rows twice more, then 1st row once. **32** (**34**-**36**-**36**-**40**-**42**) sts.
Chart XIV is now complete.

With MC only, proceed as follows:
1st row: (WS). Purl, dec **6** (**6**-**6**-**4**-**6**-**6**) sts evenly across. **26** (**28**-**30**-**32**-**34**-**36**) sts.
2nd row: K1. ssk. Knit to last 3 sts. K2tog. K1.
3rd row: Purl.
Rep last 2 rows **7** (**8**-**11**-**12**-**13**-**12**) times more. **10** (**10**-**6**-**6**-**6**-**10**) sts rem.

Sizes XS/S, M and 4/5XL only: 1st row: (RS). K1. ssk. Knit to last 3 sts. K2tog. K1.
2nd row: P1. P2tog. Purl to last 3 sts. P2togtbl. P1. 6 sts rem.

All sizes: Cast off.

FINISHING

Sew shoulder seams.

Pin all pieces to measurements. Cover with a damp cloth, leaving cloth to dry. Sew raglan seams.

Right Shawl Collar: With **WS** facing, MC and smaller needles, K**2** (**3**-**3**-**3**-**3**-**3**) from right front st holder.

1st row: (RS). Sl1. Inc 1 st in next st.

2nd and alt rows: Knit.

3rd row: Sl1. Inc 1 st in next st. Knit to end of row.

5th row: Sl1. Knit to last 2 sts. Inc 1 st in next st. Knit to end of row.

6th row: Knit.

Rep last 2 rows until there are 20 sts.

Cont even in garter st (knit every row) until Collar measures length to fit to center of Back, ending with a RS row. Break yarn. Leave sts on a spare needle.

Left Shawl Collar: With RS facing, MC and smaller needles, K**2** (**3**-**3**-**3**-**3**-**3**) from left front st holder.

1st row: (WS). Sl1. Knit to end of row.

2nd row: Inc 1 st in first st. Knit to end of row.

3rd row: Sl1. Knit to end of row.

4th row: Inc 1 st in first st. Knit to end of row.

Rep last 2 rows until there are 20 sts.

Cont even in garter st until Collar measures length to fit to center of Back, ending with a WS row. **Do not** break yarn.

3 needle cast off: Align 2 needles with Right and Left Collars facing RS tog. Knit first stitch from each needle tog. *Knit next stitch from each needle tog. Pass first st on right-hand needle over second st. Rep from * until all sts will be cast off.

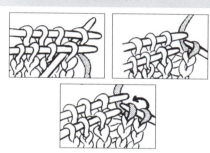

Zipper edging: With RS facing, MC and smaller needle, pick up and knit **53** (**55**-**57**-**59**-**59**-**60**) sts up Right Front to beg of neck shaping. Cast off.

Rep for Left Front. Sew zipper in position.

BERNAT

Chart VIII

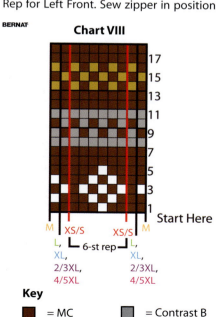

Start Here

6-st rep

Key

= MC   = Contrast B

= Contrast A   = Contrast C

Chart IX

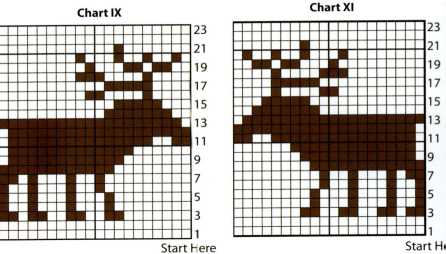

Start Here

Chart XI

Start He

Chart X

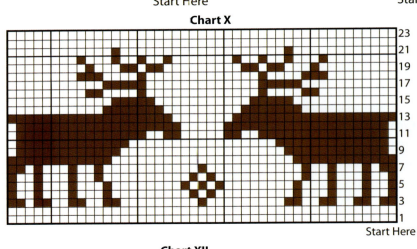

Start Here

Chart XII

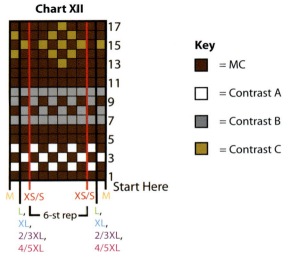

Start Here

Chart XIII (Sizes XS/S, M)

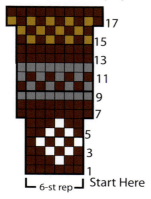

17
15
13
11
9
7
5
3
1 Start Here

6-st rep Start Here

Chart XIII (Sizes L, XL)

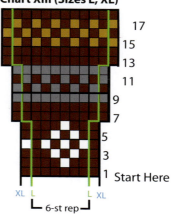

17
15
13
11
9
7
5
3
1 Start Here

XL L   L XL

6-st rep

Chart XIII (Sizes 2/3XL, 4/5XL)

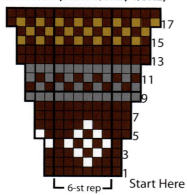

17
15
13
11
9
7
5
3
1

6-st rep Start Here

Key

 = MC

 = Contrast A

= Contrast B

= Contrast C

Chart XIV

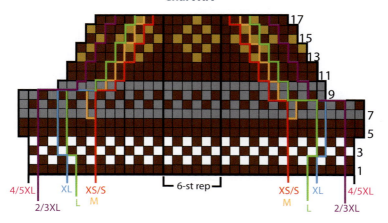

17
15
13
11
9
7
5
3
1

4/5XL   XL   XS/S   XS/S   XL   4/5XL
              M   M
2/3XL   L   6-st rep   L   2/3XL

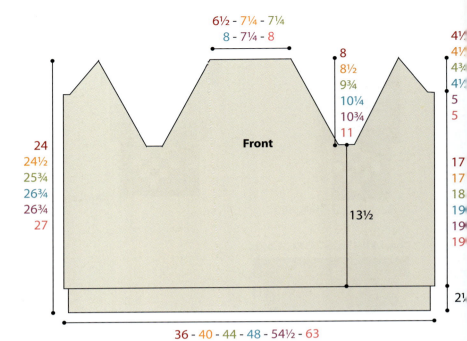

6½ - 7¼ - 7¼
8 - 7¼ - 8

8
8½
9¾
10¼
10¾
11

4½
4½
4¾
4½
5
5

Front

24
24½
25¾
26¾
26¾
27

17
17
18
19
19
19

13½

2½

36 - 40 - 44 - 48 - 54½ - 63

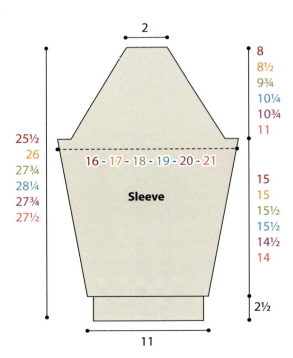

2

8
8½
9¾
10¼
10¾
11

25½
26
27¾
28¼
27¾
27½

16 - 17 - 18 - 19 - 20 - 21

Sleeve

15
15
15½
15½
14½
14

2½

11

Bernat® Softee® Chunky™

Solids/Twists: 100 g / 3.5 oz: approximately 99 m / 108 yds
Ombres: 80 g / 2.8 oz: approximately 70 m / 77 yds
100% Acrylic

WASHING AND CARE INSTRUCTIONS

Machine Washing: Wash in water (not exceeding 40°C/104°F)
at permanent press setting. Do not use bleach.
Machine Drying: Tumble dry at low heat, at delicate setting.
Do not iron or press. Do not overheat.

U.S. Knitters Please Note: Canadian and American terminologies differ slightly. Equivalents are shown.

Canadian	U.S.
cast off	bind off
tension	gauge

* = The star symbol is a repeat sign and means that you follow the printed instructions from the first * until you reach the second *. You will then repeat from * to * the given number of times which does not include the first time. The ** and *** are used in the same way.

ABBREVIATIONS

cm = centimeter(s), g = gram(s), " = inch(es), m = meter(s), mm = millimeter(s), oz = ounce(s), 0 = no stitches, times or rows

GAUGE SWATCH

For best results, be sure to use the yarn recommended in the pattern, and purchase enough of one dye lot to complete your project. It is a good idea to retain ball bands in case of inquiry. Before you begin to knit, check your gauge by making a test swatch and adjusting your needle size, if necessary, to obtain the gauge quoted in the pattern. Inaccurate gauge results in an item too large or too small. Even a variation of half a stitch makes an obvious difference in the finished size.

(Example knit gauge swatch shown: 17 sts and 21 rows).

Learn to Knit Instructions

Casting On

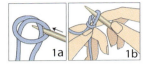

1a Make a slip knot: Loop the yarn as shown and slip needle under the lower strand of the loop.

1b Pull up a loop of yarn.

2 Pull the yarn end attached to the ball of yarn to tighten the slip knot leaving the other end approx 4 ins [10 cm] long. Transfer needle to left hand.

3a Insert the right-hand needle through slip knot and wind yarn over right-hand needle.

3b Pull loop through slip knot.

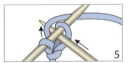

4 Place new loop on left-hand needle. [You now have 2 stitches (sts) on your left-hand needle].

5 Insert right-hand needle between last 2 stitches (sts) on left-hand needle and wind yarn over right-hand needle.

6 Pull loop through. Place this new loop on left-hand needle beside last stitch (st). (You now have 1 more stitch on left-hand needle). Repeat (rep) steps 5 and 6 until required number of stitches (sts) have been cast on left-hand needle.

The Knit Stitch

1 Hold the needle with cast on stitches (sts) in your left hand, and the loose yarn attached to the ball at the back of work. Insert right-hand needle from left to right through the front of the first stitch (st) on the left-hand needle.

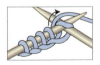

2 Wind the yarn from left to right over the point of the right-hand needle.

3 Draw the yarn through this original stitch (st) which forms a new stitch (st) on right-hand needle.

4 Slip the original stitch (st) off the left-hand needle, keeping the new stitch (st) on the right-hand needle

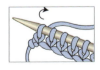

5 To knit a row, repeat steps 1 to 4 until all stitches (sts) have been transferred from left-hand needle to right-hand needle. Turn the work by transferring the needle with stitches (sts) into your left hand to knit the next row.